Profile Analysis

OXFORD PSYCHOLOGY SERIES

EDITORS

Donald E. Broadbent
James L. McGaugh
Nicholas J. Mackintosh
Michael I. Posner
Endel Tulving
Lawrence Weiskrantz

Profile Analysis
Auditory Intensity Discrimination

DAVID M. GREEN

Department of Psychology
University of Florida

OXFORD PSYCHOLOGY SERIES NO. 13

New York   Oxford
OXFORD UNIVERSITY PRESS
1988

Oxford University Press

Oxford New York Toronto
Delhi Bombay Calcutta Madras Karachi
Petaling Jaya Singapore Hong Kong Tokyo
Nairobi Dar es Salaam Cape Town
Melbourne Auckland

and associated companies in
Beirut Berlin Ibadan Nicosia

Library of Congress Cataloging-in-Publication Data
Green, David Marvin, 1932–
Profile analysis.
(Oxford psychology series ; no. 13)
Bibliography: p. Includes index.
1. Auditory perception. 2. Psychoacoustics. I. Title. II. Series.
QP465.G7 1988   152.1'5   86-18243
ISBN 0-19-504948-9

9 8 7 6 5 4 3 2 1

Printed in the United States of America
on acid-free paper

Preface

This monograph is a review of some recent research concerning the ability of normal-hearing observers to discern changes in the shape of complex acoustic spectra—what we call auditory profile analysis. It also contains a review of data on the topic of auditory intensity discrimination and the physiological mechanisms believed to be responsible for these discrimination processes. None of these topics is understood in very great detail. Our ignorance about the topic of discriminating changes in spectral shape is reasonable, since it has been the subject of systematic research for only a few years. Our ignorance about the basic mechanisms responsible for detecting a change in acoustic intensity or how those changes are coded in the nervous system is less reasonable, since it has been a central topic in physiological and psychological acoustics for nearly a half century. In both cases, better understanding of these topics would, we hope, provide a way of understanding more complex auditory skills, such as those involved in listening to music and speech. As yet, our knowledge of the more basic areas has contributed little to those more complicated domains of inquiry.

We begin with an historical review of the early experiments that led us to consider the problem of detecting a change in spectral shape. These experiments were collaborative efforts with Dr. Murray Spiegel, who, at that time, was a postdoctoral student in my laboratory. After reviewing those early beginnings, we turn to a more systematic review of the problems and issues surrounding the discrimination of a change in acoustic intensity. This review will establish some of the basic data and explain the terms and quantities used in this area. In the concluding chapters, we review in greater detail some of the factors and properties that govern our ability to hear these changes in complex acoustic signals. We conclude with a discussion of two theories about how such discriminations might be made. This first theory is a very general one, and, although obviously incomplete, it demonstrates that a theory of spectral shape discrimination is not different in kind from a theory of intensity discrimination using very simple acoustic stimuli. The second theory suggests that the discrimination between the two spectral complexes is based on a difference in pitch, which can be predicted on the basis of the weighted instantaneous frequency of the complex sounds. Thus, both theories attempt to explain spectral shape discrimination on the basis of more elementary auditory processes, but both theories use these elementary processes in complicated and intricate fashions.

I feel I must comment on the timing of this monograph. Several have asked why I undertook to summarize the research now, rather than wait a few years when our understanding will be more complete. One answer is that a goal of this review is to stimulate and encourage further effort in this area. A second, more honest answer is that, although our initial understanding may be incomplete and possibly wrong, this is the time when participation in the research is most exciting and interesting. Systematic knowledge is well and good, but the fun is in doing the experiments and even in making the mistakes that lead to a better understanding of how the auditory process works. I hope this review will convey some of the pleasure and the excitement of those initial efforts.

Last but surely not least, I wish to thank all those who helped me write and rewrite this work. Most of the research was supported by a grant from the National Institute of Health and Welfare and some of the more recent studies also enjoyed support from the Office of Scientific Research of the United States Air Force. These grants made this research possible and I thank them for their support.

Several people read and commented on individual chapters. They include Les Bernstein, Soren Buus, Larry Feth, Tom Hanna, Chris Mason, Dennis McFadden, Donna Neff, and Ginny Richards. Although I did not always take all their advice, they certainly helped improve the manuscript. Special thanks to my many collaborators, Tim Forrest, Gerald Kidd, Chris Mason, and Maria Picardi. A special thank you to Murray Spiegel whose enthusiasm and energy really started the entire enterprise. Of course, I also wish to thank those who helped in the preparation of the manuscript: Karen Fritscher, Zekiye Onsan, Arleen Pippin, and Cheryl Williams. A special thanks to Walt Jesteadt and his associates at the Boys Town National Institute for the software package GREG and the graphics programs used to plot many of the figures. Finally, I must thank Marian Heinzmann Green who helped edit and proofread the entire manuscript—only she knows where all the commas are buried.

Gainesville, Fla.   D.M.G.
August 1987

Contents

1
Early Experiments in Profile Analysis

We begin with an account of some of the early experiments—those that preceded our interest in the topic of discriminating a change in spectral shape. These experiments led us to believe that an important contributor to detection performance in these auditory masking tasks was the simultaneous comparisons of the intensity level at different parts of an acoustic spectrum. Not only were these comparisons of relative level being made, but whether or not the relative level changed from one trial to the next also influenced detection performance in ways we had not previously understood. The importance of relative level over trials also led us to consider fluctuations in the intensity levels of independent samples of random noise, because such fluctuations set the ultimate limit on any detector's ability to utilize these simultaneous comparisons. Finally, we review a more recent experiment that demonstrates the surprising effectiveness of a relatively few sinusoidal maskers. Changes in the relative level of different parts of the acoustic spectrum are described by the listener as changes in "sound quality." All the results suggest that the stability of sound quality over trials is an important factor in auditory masking experiments and this ultimately led us to systematically explore our ability to hear changes in the shape of acoustic spectra. But let us begin near the beginning.

The earliest experiments were conducted in collaboration with Dr. Murray Spiegel, a postdoctoral student, who joined my laboratory in 1979 with an NIH fellowship. He had recently completed his doctoral training with Dr. Charles Watson, working on the perception of 10-tone auditory patterns. Spiegel was anxious to convince me that the experiments he had been doing were an important new area of research in audition. Watson and his collaborators had initiated a number of investigations on the detection of a change in a single tone (either in its frequency or intensity) in the midst of a temporal stream of other tones (Watson, Wroton, Kelly, & Benbassat, 1975; Watson, 1976; Watson, Kelly, & Wroton, 1976). They had measured how the detectability of a single tone embedded in a stream of successive tones improves as either the context in which that tone occurs or the characteristics of the tone (its frequency, intensity, or position in the temporal sequence) become more and more predictable. Spiegel and I had many long and interesting discussions about this general line of research and finally began to do some experiments on masker and signal uncertainty.

We made some major changes in Watson's procedure to simplify the experimental situation. First, we presented all the tones simultaneously instead of successively. I thought that this would minimize the time it took for observers to learn the task, and I hoped that a single, static presentation would be simpler for us to understand than Watson's dynamic succession of 10 tones. In retrospect, I doubt that either task can be learned quickly; certainly neither has been easy to understand in detail. In any case, we used a single complex sound presented for 100 msec. One of the tones in the complex was increased in intensity compared to a standard condition, and the observer's task was to detect that increment. This is, fundamentally, an intensity discrimination task, since the observer must say whether a given tone was at one level, that of the standard, or a different level, that of the standard plus the increment. The other tones of the complex were always presented at the same intensity level. One can regard these equal-energy components as maskers that obscure whether or not the signal component has been increased in intensity. In practice, we used a two-alternative forced-choice procedure—the observer heard two brief sounds: one was the standard (or masker), which was a collection of equal-intensity components, and the other sound was the same standard with an increment (signal) added to just one component of the complex. The observer tried to select the interval that contained the signal.

Spiegel and I collaborated on several experiments. The results were often surprising and, in order to explore these new results more fully, only some selected results of those investigations will be presented in this review. In our first experiment, we used sets of complex tones as the masker and varied the frequency uncertainty of both the signal and masker. In later experiments, we investigated the effects of uncertainty about the signal frequency using a noise masker. We also varied the duration of the presentation, because this manipulates the stability of the noise spectrum. For reasons that will gradually become clear, we also randomized the overall level of the sounds presented in the two intervals.

SIGNAL AND MASKER UNCERTAINTY

In our first experiment, we used sinusoids as the set of potential maskers and constructed the actual maskers used in a specific experimental condition by drawing from this larger set of tones. The larger set consisted of 200 sinusoids, all equal in amplitude and in logarithmic frequency spacing over the interval from 300 to 3000 Hz. Thus, the first tone had a frequency of 300 Hz, the second had a frequency of 303.5 Hz, the next about 307 Hz, and so forth. The one hundredth tone, the middle of the range, had a frequency of about 948.6 Hz, and the last tone had a frequency of 3000 Hz.

The 12-tone scale of Western music employs 12 tones per octave, which corresponds to a frequency ratio of about 1.059 between successive tones of the scale. We had 200 tones in about 3½ octaves, which corresponds to a frequency ratio of about 1.012. In effect, we had nearly a 60-tone scale. For a given experimental condition, we selected from this set of 200 tones a subset of n ($n = 1$ to 20) components for use as the masker for a block of several hundred trials. In the two-alternative forced-choice task, the masker alone was presented in one interval and in the other interval a tone, the signal, was added (in-phase) to one component of the masker. Thus, in one interval, the component was presented at the standard amplitude, A, and in the other, it was presented at an amplitude, $\Delta A + A$. The observer's task was to select the interval containing the increment, ΔA. We measured the threshold of the increment in this situation by using an adaptive psychophysical procedure. The adaptive rule leads to a signal level that corresponds to about 70.7% correct in the two-alternative task. The dependent variable of the experiment was the threshold value of this increment relative to the standard in decibels, 20 log ($\Delta A/A$). All the sounds were generated by a computer and were presented for a 100-msec duration with a 5-msec rise and fall. The standard tones were presented at a level of about 60 dB SPL.

The data we will present consist of the results obtained in four experimental conditions. These four conditions are created by either fixing or randomizing the frequency of the signal or masker(s) on each trial of the forced-choice task. Let us describe these conditions in detail.

(a) Fixed signal–fixed masker

The frequency of the signal was fixed, as were the n components of the masker ($n = 1$ to 20). If $n = 1$, there was a single sinusoid of fixed frequency presented on each trial. Its amplitude was either A or $\Delta A + A$ and we were measuring the conventional Weber fraction for a sinusoid. If $n > 1$, then on every trial the same set of several tones was present, but one of the tones, also fixed over trials, was increased in level in the signal interval.

(b) Fixed signal–random masker

The n components of the masker were drawn at random from the set of 200 tones on each trial. The observer heard the same n components in each of the two intervals in the forced-choice trial, but the specific n components changed on every trial. A single component of the masker was fixed in frequency—the one to which the signal may be added. The signal was initially presented at a clearly detectable level so that the frequency of this signal component was known to the observer. Since the signal was fixed in frequency, when $n = 1$, this condition was the same as (a) above.

(c) Random signal–fixed masker

The n components of the masker were drawn from the set of 200 tones and held fixed for several blocks of one hundred trials. On each trial, the signal frequency was chosen at random from this set of n components and the increment was added to that component. This is formally similar to the older detection experiments on the effects of signal uncertainty in noise. If $n = 1$, then this condition was identical to condition (a) above.

(d) Random signal–random masker

Both signal and masker changed in frequency from trial to trial. The n components of the masker were drawn from the set of 200 tones. On a single trial, one of the components of the masker was selected at random as the signal frequency and the increment was added to that tone. The observer heard the same n tones presented in the two intervals of the forced-choice procedure, but one of these tones was presented at a larger amplitude in one of the intervals. If $n = 1$, then this condition is similar to condition (a) above, except that the frequency of the single sinusoid changes from trial to trial.

Figure 1-1, which is Figure 2 of Spiegel, Picardi, and Green (1981), shows the results of this experiment. The abscissa of the graph is the number of components heard on any single trial, n. The ordinate is the threshold for the increment measured in terms of the signal level re the level of the component to which it was added. The different symbols on the graph code the four different conditions of the experiment. For all four conditions, as one might expect, the more components in the masker the more difficult it was to hear the increment added to a single one.

We should observe that, although this result is consistent with our intuitions, it depends on the fact that the frequencies of the components in the masker are chosen at random. Thus, as the number of components increases, more and more masker components may fall in a frequency region near the signal. This will increase the amount of masking, as anyone familiar with the critical band concept should recognize. Later, we will report on studies where the components of the complex masker are spaced regularly throughout the spectrum. In these studies, as one increases the number of components, the detection of the increment will initially improve as we add more components to the complex background

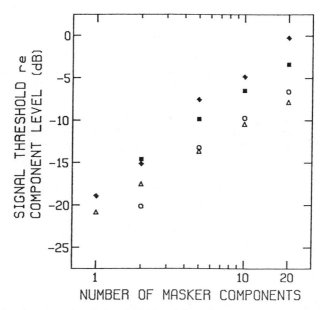

Figure 1-1. Average signal threshold levels as a function of the number of components in the masker for four conditions. The symbols for the four conditions are: fixed signal–fixed masker (open triangle), fixed signal–random masker (solid square), random signal–fixed masker (open circle), and random signal–random masker (solid diamond). (Data taken from Spiegel, Picardi, & Green, 1981.)

spectra. A second point to note about the present data is that for any value for n, the number of tones, the condition with the least uncertainty (fixed signal–fixed masker) is superior to the condition with the most uncertainty (random signal–random masker).

We should also note that only two points are plotted for $n = 1$. The tasks are both simple intensity discrimination of a single pure tone, but in one condition the frequency of the tone was fixed, while in the other the tone was randomly selected from trial to trial. Over the frequency range studied, there is little change in the Weber fraction as a function of the frequency of the sinusoid (Jesteadt, Wier, & Green, 1977). As is usual, uncertainty about any signal parameter makes detection performance worse, but the deterioration in detection performance is only 1 or 2 dB.

What is surprising about the single-component data of Figure 1-1 is that randomizing the masker produced poorer performance than randomizing the signal, that is, square symbols are always above the circles. This is unexpected because, from one point of view, there is no reason to expect that masker uncertainty would have any effect whatsoever. Compare first the conditions as we change the number of tones from one to two, as shown in Figure 1-1. If the signal is randomized holding the masker fixed, then the increase in threshold is only about one decibel (open triangle to open circle). Now make the same comparison if we add another, random-frequency, component to the complex but hold the signal frequency fixed. The increase in threshold is about six decibels (open circle or solid diamond to solid square). This comparison captures the essential results of the experiment. It is easier to hear an increment when it is added to either one of two tones fixed in frequency than to hear the same increment when added to a fixed tone if another tone is present whose frequency is chosen at random. The basic problem is why the random-frequency tone has any effect whatsoever. It is, after all, irrelevant to the task of detecting the increment on the fixed tone. From the viewpoint of the critical band, the random-frequency tone should only influence the detection of the increment when the two tones are close enough together to produce some masking. Given the way our tones are selected, this happens rarely and, even when it does occur, the effect should be small because, at worst, the two tones, when close in frequency, will simply produce a somewhat larger standard against which the increment must be detected.

A different way to summarize the results is the following. While this description hardly qualifies as an explanation, it does capture what we feel is a critical feature of this experiment. The tone of random frequency changes the quality of the sound heard from trial to trial, and these changes in quality make it difficult to compare the intensity levels in the two temporal intervals. It is similar to the difficulty one has in trying to judge the brightness of two colors that differ in wavelength. The salient dimension is the hue, not the brightness, and this makes relative judgments on the secondary dimension difficult. This summary captures what we feel is the essential message of the experiment. When the two frequencies are fixed, as in the random-signal condition, the sound quality is the same and whether the increase in intensity occurs on one component or another is not critical. In the other condition, only one tone is fixed in frequency, the other tone, the masker, changes frequency from trial to trial. This variation in masker frequency changes the quality of the sound and makes a judgment about the intensity of the second tone difficult. The random-masker condition, with its ever-changing tonal quality, makes it difficult to compare intensity levels and, hence, causes the effect of masker uncertainty to be larger than the effect of signal uncertainty at all values of n. But why is it so easy to compare intensity levels when the frequency of the components are fixed (random signal–fixed masker)?

Let us explore these remarks about sound quality in more detail and consider a logical but extreme extension of this position. Consider the condition we discussed earlier—an increment in one or the other component of two fixed-frequency components (random signal–fixed masker, $n = 2$). If a simultaneous comparison is made between the levels of the two components of the spectrum, then the observer is simply trying to determine if two tones are equal in level or different. The absolute level of neither component is important, only the relative level. In effect, we are asking if a line connecting the top of the two lines of the spectrum is flat or tilts. Therefore, suppose we were to randomize the level of the sound on each presentation. A relative comparison of the two tones should be unaffected by such a manipulation, and the threshold for the increment to the single tone should be the same even if the overall level of both tones changes from trial to trial or, indeed, from observation interval to observation interval with a single trial.

This curious prediction was the essential idea behind the final experiment. We repeated the experiment on signal and masker uncertainty, but the level of the sound on any single presentation was a random variable. We chose that level from a uniform distribution of intensities, in 1 dB steps, from either a range of 40 dB in one condition or 60 dB in a second condition. The center of the range was always 50 dB SPL. For all four uncertainty conditions, the effect of randomizing the overall level did have an effect; namely, it made the increment harder to hear by about 5 dB when the range was 40 dB and about 6 dB when the range was 60 dB. In a separate, control experiment, we forced the observers to listen *solely* to absolute level. We did this by placing the increment on *all* components of the complex. In that condition, the measured increase in threshold was about 19 dB for the 40-dB range and about 26 dB for the 60-dB range. There is, of course, no change in spectral shape if the increment is added to all components. The measured increase of only 5 to 6 dB in the main experimental conditions convinced us that the observers must be listening to changes in the shape of the spectrum, not simply absolute level. Detecting a change in spectral shape depends on making simultaneous comparisons of level from different regions of the spectrum. This experiment convinced us that these simultaneous comparisons of level were much more important than had been previously believed.

The effects of uncertainty were much the same as we had found in the original fixed-level experiment. Again, the best of the four conditions was the one with no uncertainty, the worst was the one with the most uncertainty, and those of intermediate uncertainty produced intermediate thresholds. In this experiment with random presentation levels, signal and masker uncertainty were approximately equal in their effect.

Before leaving these results, there is one final point to be discussed. It concerns the results obtained when we randomized the overall level of the masker and added the increment to *all* components of the masker. This manipulation means that overall level is the only cue one can use to detect the signal. What would one expect the results of fluctuation in overall level to be for a detector that bases its decision solely on differences in overall level? In short, what is the optimum detection performance in such a situation? Appendix A analyzes this question in detail and Figure 1-4 shows exactly how the signal-to-standard level should change as the overall level is varied over a rectangular distribution of intensity levels. A surprising outcome of this calculation is that our experimental results for the condition in which we force the observer to listen only to level—the increase of 19 and 26 dB cited above—are actually about 10 dB worse than what we would have expected from this optimum calculation.

Why are the observed values so much greater than what we calculate? We believe it is because the observers are trying to make simultaneous comparisons between different parts of the spectrum—as they had presumably done in most of the other experimental conditions. Indeed, one might say that we had been teaching the observers that a means of avoiding the effects of changes in overall level was to make such simultaneous comparisons. In this particular case, however, because the increment is placed on all of the components of the complex, such a comparison is futile and a decision based on successive comparisons of level would be more effective. Naturally, if you change the experimental task (e.g., by requiring the observer to detect an increment in a single sinusoid that varies in overall level), then the observed data must and do fall very close to the theoretical curve. But one must keep in mind that in any experimental task the observer is learning a set of detection skills that may be appropriate only for a limited set of conditions. Unless extensive training is devoted to each particular condition, it is not surprising that the obtained thresholds are worse than the optimum calculation based on the cues most relevant to the specific task.

SIGNAL AND MASKER UNCERTAINTY— NOISE MASKERS

The results with pure-tone maskers on the effect of different amounts and kinds of uncertainty led us to repeat these experiments using a different kind of masker (Spiegel & Green, 1982). Tonal maskers, especially when only a few tones are used, sound quite different from noise maskers. When listening to random tonal maskers involving only a few components, one cannot help being struck by the quite different sound qualities produced on different trials by the changing tones. With noise maskers, on the other hand, although the actual distribution of energy does change over trials, the phenomenal impression remains remarkably constant. The noise maintains a constant, hissy quality that changes little with time. Would the effects of signal uncertainty be present for maskers whose quality is more stable over trials?

To make the conditions comparable to those used with tonal maskers, we used digitally constructed noise samples so that they could be repeated exactly over a set of trials, just as we used the tonal components to repeat the same spectra on repeated trials. These "frozen noise" samples could then be fixed for a set of trials or changed from trial to trial, as we had changed the set of tonal maskers in the random-masker conditions. We should note that even when the noise changed from trial to trial the same noise waveform was used in both observation intervals of the forced-choice trial. As it had been in the previous experiment, the signal could either be fixed in frequency or randomized over trials. The signal was added incoherently to the digital noise sample. Thus, unlike the previous experiment, adding the signal to the noise might produce an increment or decrement in the spectral level in the region of the signal frequency because the noise might be in or out of phase with the signal. We also varied the bandwidth, duration, and center frequency of the noise band. We will ignore these manipulations in the following summary, since they are not directly related to our present purpose.

In this noise experiment, the signal or masker uncertainty had about the same effect as it did with the tonal maskers. Both signal and masker uncertainty produced the highest thresholds; fixing both signal and masker produced the lowest thresholds; and signal or masker uncertainty alone produced very similar results. Thus, the results obtained with tonal maskers are also true of noise maskers, despite the obvious differences in the sound quality of the two kind of maskers.

Again, we interpret this outcome as evidence for a simultaneous comparison of level in different parts of the spectrum. Such a relative comparison would explain why the effects of signal uncertainty were not larger and why masker uncertainty produced any effect at all. Once more, we ran some conditions in which we randomized the overall level of the presentations to demonstrate the importance of these simultaneous comparisons. One set of results nicely summarizes our main conclusion. Table 1-1 shows the results obtained when we compared the two extreme conditions of uncertainty with either a fixed overall level or an overall level that changed over a 40-dB interval.

Note that for the fixed signal–fixed masker condition, because the signal duration is about one-tenth second, the signal energy re noise power density is about 5 dB. This value is 5 dB better than the usual number for a sinusoid in random noise, presumably because the noise is fixed and held constant for a number of trials. For this same condition, varying the level of the presentation over a 40-dB range increased the threshold only

Table 1-1. Variation in masker level for two conditions

Overall Masker Level	Fixed Signal and Fixed Masker	Random Signal and Random Masker
Fixed	15.2 ± 2.0	22.0 ± 1.4
40-dB range	18.1 ± 1.0	23.0 ± 1.3

Note: Entries are average threshold values in decibels for three observers, expressed as signal power level to masker spectrum level.

about 3 dB. If the absolute intensity level in the critical band were the only cue used by the observer in this task, then a variation of 40 dB in overall level should cause an increase in the fixed level threshold by nearly 25 dB (5 dB from Figure 1-4 and 20 dB assuming the critical band is 100 Hz wide). For the random condition, the increase in threshold caused by the randomization of presentation level was only 1 dB. Clearly, these results demonstrate that observers are using something other than *successive* comparisons of the overall intensity level of the two sounds to detect the signal. One way to avoid the effects of randomization of the overall level is to make relative comparisons of intensity levels in different parts of the spectrum. These relative comparisons will be unaffected by changes in overall level. We will describe these relative comparisons of spectral levels as a *simultaneous* comparison level to contrast them with the *successive* comparisons that can be made by comparing the level of one sound with another over time. We will explore this simultaneous comparison process in more detail in later chapters. For the present, let us consider another aspect of this problem: how fluctuations in the noise level from trial to trial influence a detector trying to make such relative comparison.

NOISE LEVEL FLUCTUATION

In the experiment just discussed, the noise samples were stored in a computer. For the fixed-noise conditions, the same masker waveform was presented on each and every trial of the 50-trial block. One interval of the forced-choice task would contain the noise waveform alone; the other interval would contain that same noise waveform with a signal added to it. Such noise is a deterministic waveform, that is, a digital sample of noise that is repeated. Thus, even if the overall level is changing from presentation to presentation, the difference in level between different parts of the spectrum is independent of overall level. Hence, it is rational to use such differences in level as a cue for detecting the presence or absence of the signal. The level difference will be one value if the signal is present and another value if it is not.

The question we wish to address is whether such relative level comparisons are effective cues for detecting signals added to ordinary random noise. Because ordinary noise waveforms are random and unpredictable, one might think that relative comparisons between different spectral regions would be pointless. Like most things, this is a matter of degree, and in this section we will calculate the fluctuations in spectral level of random noise and how the size of such fluctuations depends on the duration and the bandwidth of the noise process.

Let us be clear at the outset about what we are trying to calculate. Suppose we had two independent samples of a noise process. The duration of each noise waveform is T seconds, and we are interested in the power in a band of frequencies W Hz wide. If we calculate this power in decibels, it would be called the power level of the noise in a bandwidth W when sampled for a duration T. How much does this power level fluctuate for independent samples of noise?

To calculate the power fluctuations in such a noise process, we assume that the noise can be adequately approximated by a finite set of sinusoidal components. For most purposes, this assumption seems to be sufficiently accurate and we will not expand further on it. Specifically, we will assume that a noise sample of bandwidth W and duration T can be represented by $2WT$ sinusoidal components. For example, the first and second components have a frequency of $(1/T)$—one component is in sine phase, and the other in cosine phase. The third (sine) and fourth (cosine) components have a frequency of $(2/T)$, and so forth. All components in this representation are orthogonal, that is, their cross product, integrated over the interval T, is exactly zero. The band need not extend from 0 to W Hz; it could also be a bandpass process having bandwidth W Hz.

At this point, we could begin a long, mathematical derivation of the absolute level of various quantities of the noise process and their variability. For those interested in these absolute values, consult Green and Swets (1966) or Blackman and Tukey (1959). Since we are interested only in the relative variability, we can shorten these derivations. The kernel of the following arguments depends on observing a number of similarities between certain statistical quantities and characteristics of the noise process. To make this parallelism obvious, we have listed the physical and statistical facts. Central to all our assertions is that the amplitudes of the components in our representation of the noise process are Gaussian random variables. Furthermore, these amplitudes are all independent of each other, both statistically and physically.

Physical Fact	Statistical Fact
The energy of a sinusoid is proportional to the square of its amplitude.	The square of a normalized Gaussian random variable is chi-square distributed with one degree of freedom.
The total energy in a band, W, is the sum of the energy of individual components, if the components are independent.	The sum of m independent chi-square variables is also chi-square distributed with m degrees of freedom.

The total energy in a band W is proportional to that chi-square variable with m degrees of freedom. The total number of independent components in a band W is $2WT$, because the components are spaced $1/T$ apart and there are two components at each frequency. Thus, the total energy in a band W sampled from a noise waveform of duration, T seconds, is chi-square distributed with $2WT$ degrees of freedom. The fluctuations in such a sample can be calculated simply from the mean and variance of the chi-square distribution.

Statistical fact

The mean of a chi-square variable is equal to the degrees of freedom; the variance is equal to twice the degrees of freedom. Hence, the coefficient of variation (the mean divided by the standard deviation) is the square root of one-half the degrees of freedom.

The coefficient of variation for the power of independent samples of a noise waveform when measured in a band W based on a waveform duration T is thus

$$\text{Coefficient of variation} = (WT)^{1/2} \qquad \text{Eq. 1.1}$$

To estimate the exact size of these fluctuations, one must make some assumptions concerning the integration time of the ear and the width of the critical band filter. If we assume an integration time of 100 msec and a critical bandwidth of 100 Hz at a center frequency of 1000 Hz, then the WT product is 10 and the coefficient of variation is about 3. If the mean power is three, fluctuation of one sigma unit will range between 2 and 4 power units. Converting to decibels (it is convenient to use 3 power units as our reference power), the mean level is 0 dB and a one sigma fluctuation above or below the mean corresponds to plus 1.25 db and minus 1.76 db, respectively. For a one-tenth second sample of noise at moderate frequencies, the amount of fluctuation in the spectral level of the noise is only a few decibels.

The following conclusion can be drawn from such calculations. A process that calculates the power in two distinct frequency bands and compares their relative levels should be able to detect changes in *spectral shape,* if these changes are a bit larger than a few decibels created by the natural fluctuations in the noise process. Such a comparison process would be unaffected by changes in overall level, since the critical comparison is a simultaneous comparison of the level in two different frequency bands. Such a detection process would generate data similar to what Spiegel and Green (1982) observed when they randomized the overall level of the sound by 40 dB (see Table 1-1).

To assess the potency of such a relative comparison process and to explore how detection changes as we vary the frequency region where the changes in spectral shape occur, we recently conducted a set of experiments exploring the detection of a 100-msec sinusoidal signal presented in a broadband noise. In different conditions, the frequency of the signal was varied from 500 to 6000 Hz. In one condition, the noise was fixed in level at 70 dB SPL. In the other condition, the *mean* level was 70 dB, but the level on each presentation was varied randomly over a 40-dB range

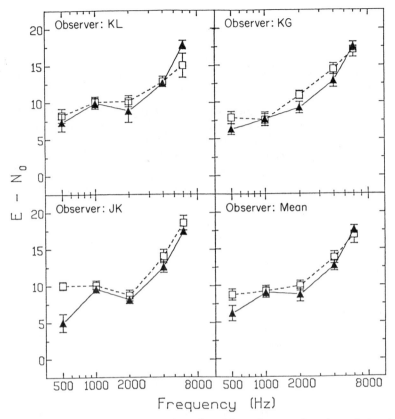

Figure 1-2. Threshold for sinusoidal signal in noise as a function of signal frequency for three observers and their average. The abscissa is the signal frequency in cycles per second (Hz). The ordinate is the signal energy to noise power density. Two conditions are displayed. In one condition, the overall noise level is fixed at 70 dB SPL (solid traingles). In the other, the level of the noise on each presentation varies randomly over a 40-dB range (open squares).

in 1-dB steps. Thus, the first interval might contain a sound presented at an overall level of 43 dB, whereas the second interval might contain a sound presented at 76 dB. The observer's task was to select the interval in which a sinusoid had been added to the noise. We adjusted the amplitude of the sinusoid, so that it was detected with a probability of about 0.707. The results obtained with the fixed (solid triangles) and random presentation level (open squares) are shown in Figure 1-2. Three observers' results are shown in three panels of the figure as well as the average over the three observers in the fourth panel. In almost every case, randomizing the level of presentation produces somewhat higher thresholds for detecting the sinusoid, but the difference is rarely as much as 2 dB. Clearly, subjects in this task can detect the presence of the sinusoid on the basis of *relative* energy level at different parts of the spectrum. They are not forced to make decisions about the presence or absence of the sinusoidal signal on the basis of *absolute* energy levels.

Those familiar with psychoacoustic research will recognize that the fixed condition of the experiment we just described is a replication of part of the now-classic study by Hawkins and Stevens (1950). These researchers would, I am sure, have been disturbed had the power amplifier in their experiment broken and varied in gain over a 40-dB range from one presentation to the next. These are exactly the random conditions in our study. Hawkins and Stevens would have fixed the amplifier, as I am sure all of us would. The surprising fact is that this particular failure would have made little difference in the results of their experiment. In terms of the average results at 1000 Hz, the random conditions produce almost the same critical ratio as the fixed conditions.

HOW MANY SINUSOIDAL MASKERS MAKE A NOISE?

In the preceding sections, we noted that the effects of signal/masker uncertainty were similar whether we used multicomponent sinusoids or broadband noise as the masker. We have also noted that the phenomenal impressions created by these two stimuli are very different. Unless a great many sinusoidal components are used, a multicomponent sinusoid has a tonal character that is quite different from the atonal, hissy quality of a broadband noise. On the other hand, we know that if a large number of sinusoidal components is used, one can simulate broadband noise very closely both in a mathematical and phenomenal sense. This leads us to the question of how many sinusoidal components must be used to achieve the same masking effectiveness as a broadband noise. Mathematically, we have already observed that if we have a noise bandwidth of W and a duration T, then $2WT$ components can be used to approximate a noise waveform very closely. This was the approximation used in the preceding section and it is based on the so-called Nyquist rate. For a 10,000-Hz bandwidth and a one-tenth second duration, the number is 2000 components. But does one actually need all these components to approximate the masking effectiveness of noise?

In vision, Richards (1979) has suggested, and others have confirmed, that only a few sinusoidal grating components, 10 or fewer, are needed to achieve the same visual appearance as a random noise pattern. It would be interesting to determine this number for an auditory masking experiment. Is this number near 10 or near the much larger number suggested by the Nyquist rate? This was the essential motivation of a small study carried out by Neff and Green (1986). The results were somewhat surprising but not so difficult to understand, given the results of the studies on masker uncertainty reviewed earlier.

The design of the experiment was straightforward. The signal to be detected is a sinusoid of fixed frequency. Three signal frequencies, 250, 1000, and 4000 Hz, were used in different experimental conditions. The masker was either (1) a broadband (5000 Hz) noise stimulus of fixed noise power density or (2) a multicomponent sinusoidal complex. The frequency composition of the multitonal masker was randomized for each of the intervals in the forced-choice test. The frequency of each component of the complex was chosen at random from the frequency interval occupied by the noise, 0 to 5000 Hz, except that no components were allowed to fall in a 10-Hz interval about the signal frequency. The components were all Gaussian in amplitude, with the same fixed variance. The independent variable of the experiment was the number of components in the sinusoidal complex. The dependent variable was the threshold for the signal.

Figure 1-3 shows the results obtained at each signal frequency. The data are the average thresholds obtained for three observers. The points plot-

Figure 1-3. The amount of masking (elevation in threshold) caused by using different numbers of randomly chosen, sinusoidal maskers. Three different signal frequencies are indicated by different symbols. The data are average thresholds over three listeners. The total power of the masker is held constant as the number of components is varied. The masking produced by a broadband noise of that same total power is coded by the symbol encompassing the letter *N* for each signal frequency.

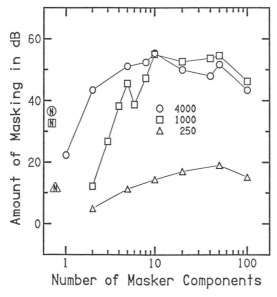

ted at the left side of the graph enclosing the letter N are the results obtained when the masker is a broadband noise. As might be expected, increasing the number of masking components leads to more masking, at least initially. A very few components, 2 to 4 depending on the frequency of the signal, are sufficient to equal or achieve the masking produced by a broadband noise. Adding more components than this minimal amount produces more masking than can be achieved with the noise, as much as 10 to 15 dB more masking for the higher frequency signals. Finally, as the number of components increases, a clear decline in the amount of masking is seen.

If one listens to these different conditions, the results are not unexpected. If only a single sinusoid is used, the masking is not very great, because the masker and signal are often widely separated in frequency and the presence of the signal is not difficult to hear. If the number of components exceeds 20 or 30, the individual components become more difficult to detect, and the masker appears to become more similar from one presentation to the next. With 30 or more components comprising the masker, the addition of the signal to the masker sounds much the same, independent of the particular components used in the masker. At an intermediate number of components, the task is much more difficult, because the individual components of the masking complex are resolved and the changing frequency composition of the masker makes it difficult to determine what the signal should sound like, except at very high signal levels.

Admittedly, the previous description is simply a post-hoc account of the empirical results. Were the results quite different, then different rationalizations would be proposed. We do, however, believe this account emphasizes what is a common thread of this chapter; namely, that the signal is detected on the basis of a qualitative change in the character of the masker. This quality is determined by a simultaneous comparison of different parts of the frequency spectrum. Conditions that produce large changes in the quality of the sound from one presentation to the next prevent the observer from making these simultaneous comparisons and, hence, lead to greater amounts of masking. Maskers that are relatively constant in quality, and by this phrase we mean maskers whose relative levels at different frequency regions are relatively stable over time, allow one to detect smaller changes in the spectrum.

This summary emphasizes that simultaneous comparisons of different spectral levels can and are used in masking experiments. Such comparisons have heretofore been virtually ignored by most previous accounts of the masking process; rather, the stress has been given to successive comparison of levels. Successive comparison is also important in the detection process, but the utilization of such cues occurs when simultaneous comparison is impossible. Successive comparison occurs when the sounds to be compared have similar sound qualities, that is, their spectral shapes are similar and simultaneous comparison is impossible.

APPENDIX A
Effects of overall level fluctuation

In this appendix, we derive the equations that tell us how the amount of random variation in the overall sound level should influence the detection of an increment in a two-alternative forced-choice ($2AFC$) task. Specifically, we assume the two levels are measured, L_1 and L_2, in the two intervals of the forced-choice test. The decision rule is to select the interval containing the larger level as the interval containing the increment. We denote the two stimuli as having pressures, x and y, where $y = x(1 + \Delta)$. Thus, y is larger than x by an increment Δ. The decibel difference between the two sounds is $C = 20 \log (1 + \Delta)$. If this quantity, C, were a threshold value, it would be called the level difference in decibels, denoted ΔL (see Chapter 3). Now we suppose that each sound is varied in overall level. This perturbation in level is rectangularly distributed in decibels over a range of R dB. How does the range of variation, R, affect the percentage of correct detections of the increment, Δ, given this simple decision rule?

We use X to represent the decibel level of the smaller stimulus and Y for the decibel level of the larger. Since they are rectangularly distributed over a range R, the distribution of X is

$$P(X < t) = t/R \qquad 0 < t < R \qquad \text{Eq. A.1}$$

or its density is

$$f_X(t) = 1/R \qquad 0 < t < R \qquad \text{Eq. A.2}$$

The distribution of Y is similar to that of X except that it is shifted by an amount C; that is, it ranges from C to $R + C$.

The probability of being correct in $2AFC$ is the probability of the sample of Y being greater than the sample of X. This probability could be calculated in many ways. A straightforward approach is to note that this probability is equal to the probability that X is less than Y for a fixed value for Y and then integrate over all possible values for Y, that is,

$$P(X < Y) = \int P(X < Y)P(Y = t)\, dt \qquad \text{Eq. A.3}$$

Next, we must consider the limits of integration. The variable of integration, t, must be considered in three possible regions: (1) $t < C$, (2) $C < t < R$, and (3) $t > R$. For the first region, $t < c$, the probability of Y being equal to t in the interval 0 to C is zero, so we can start the lower limit of integration at C. For the third region, $t > R$, if t is greater than R, then X must be less than Y and this happens with probability C/R, so we might simply add that probability and calculate the integral only over the second region, namely, for t between C and R.

$$P(X < Y) = C/R + \int_{C}^{R} (t/R)(1/R)\, dt \qquad \text{Eq. A.4}$$

This integral is easy to evaluate. It is

$$P(X < Y) = C/R + (1/R^2)(1/2)t^2 \Big|_C^R$$

$$= C/R + \frac{1}{2} - \frac{1}{2}(C/R)^2$$

Eq. A.5

The probability of a correct answer is a quadratic equation in C/R. If we use an adaptive procedure, it will track a probability level PL equal to $P(X < Y)$. Thus, if we solve the quadratic equation, we find

$$C/R = 1 - 2^{1/2}(1 - PL)^{1/2}$$

Eq. A.6

In most of our adaptive experiments, we use the 2-down 1-up procedure which tracks a probability level, PL, of 0.707. For this adaptive procedure, substituting PL = 0.707 in Eq. A.6, we find C/R = .2346. The level difference in decibels expected for a range, R, is then simply 0.2346 times R. If different adaptive rules are used, then different values of PL

Figure 1-4. The expected threshold for the signal as a function of the range of level variation used for the masker, if absolute level is the only cue used to detect the signal. The abscissa is the range of rectangular variation in level of the standard. The ordinate is threshold value (signal-to-standard ratio in dB) for the three adaptive procedures indicated.

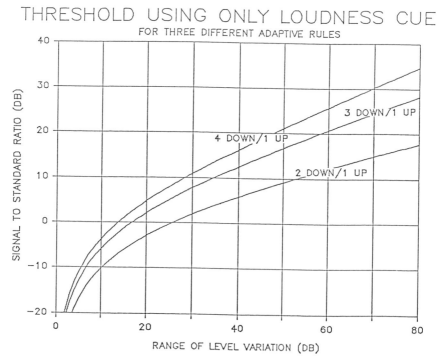

THRESHOLD USING ONLY LOUDNESS CUE
FOR THREE DIFFERENT ADAPTIVE RULES

will obtain, and the proportionality constant relating C and R can be computed from Eq. A.6.

In Figure 1-4 we have converted the value of C, the level difference in decibels, to the signal-to-standard ratio that we have often used to measure the threshold value for the signal. This measure of signal threshold is plotted as a function of the range of variation, R, for three simple adaptive rules. These rules are the 2-down 1-up rule, which tracks a probability level of 0.707, the 3-down 1-up rule, which tracks PL $= 0.7937$, and the 4-down 1-up rule, which tracks PL $= 0.8409$. These three different probability levels are marked in Figure 1-4. As can be seen from the figure, an overall range of 40 dB should require a signal-to-standard level of 5 dB for the 2-down 1-up rule. Using the same adaptive rule, a range of 80 dB should increase that level to about 18 dB. With smaller ranges of fluctuation, the effect of randomizing overall level yields much lower thresholds. For example, a range of 10 dB only increases the signal-to-standard level -10 dB. This fact is unfortunate from an experimental point of view. If the threshold for detecting a change in spectral shape is relatively poor, then one must employ a large range of fluctuation in overall level to eliminate absolute level as an effective cue. Sometimes such a large range of variation in overall level is impractical. For example, if one uses these techniques with someone whose hearing is abnormal, the absolute threshold for that individual may be initially large and the limited range of hearing prevents one from using a very large range of fluctuation in overall level. For such cases, it may be desirable to modify an adaptive rule that tracks a higher probability level. Rules of this type are illustrated in the figure. Each rule yields a higher expected threshold, when detection is based on the level cue alone. Thus, one can be certain that a threshold significantly less than the value indicated in the figure is based on the detection of changes in spectral shape rather than changes in absolute level. When studying the detection of changes in spectral shape, one notes that these curves define ceiling effects, and adaptive techniques that track higher probability level provide some amelioration of the limitations imposed by these ceilings.

2

Intensity Discrimination

One of the most basic auditory skills is the ability to detect a change in the intensity of a sound. The discrimination of a change in intensity is helpful in a variety of situations. One can use such information to decide whether a sound source is approaching or receding. The intensity level of a familiar sound can be used to infer the distance of the source. Although our speech does not employ changes in intensity as part of the phonetic code, emphasis and stress can only be understood by making distinctions among the relative intensities of different words of the speaker. Certainly, one would suppose that this fundamental and elementary auditory ability would be understood in considerable detail, and that the physiological mechanism supporting this basic discrimination would also be well understood.

This is not the case. At practically every level of discourse, there are serious theoretical problems that prevent offering a complete explanation of how the discrimination of a change in intensity is accomplished. These difficulties are illustrated in our understanding of the physiological mechanisms. Although everyone agrees that increases in intensity cause increases in neural firing rates, there are serious problems in claiming that such changes are the sole code for signaling changes in intensity, at least over the entire dynamic range of hearing. Early ideas have been overturned, and there is still no consensus on the proper explanation. Despite this ignorance on the physiological level, one might expect that since reasonably accurate descriptions of intensity discrimination data exist, there would be more molar, psychoacoustic models that could predict the data. Here, also, our earlier ideas have been overturned, and there is little consensus about the new suggestions. Even summary descriptions of the data are rather untidy. Weber's law, the simplest rule, says that an intensity change will be noticed when the stimulus changes a certain ratio of its present amount. This rule is almost exactly true for many sensory attributes in several different sensory modalities. It is also true for certain auditory stimuli such as wide-band noise. But it is clearly an inadequate description of the data on the detection of a change in the intensity of the premier auditory stimulus, the sinusoid.

This monograph is a description of these problems and our attempts to understand how this very basic auditory discrimination is accomplished. The particular impetus for this review was a recent series of experiments conducted in our laboratory. The task was to detect a change in the intensity of a single component in a multitonal complex. Because the task is to detect whether the spectrum is flat or has a slight bump, we have called this kind of discrimination task "profile analysis." Given the traditional view of intensity discrimination, the results of these experiments were very unexpected. Many seemed to contradict some of our most cherished ideas about how intensity discrimination works.

We begin with a review of past research on the topic of intensity discrimination. The traditional view of the process will be explained, and we will also describe some of our recent results using profile analysis. In the following chapters, we will review, in more detail, specific intensity discrimination tasks and summarize the empirical data available in these areas. Although we are not able to provide a simple mechanism that can account for all the diverse results, we hope this survey will indicate the major empirical data available in each area and help to make some future synthesis possible.

SIMPLE RATE MODELS: POISSON STATISTICS

The simplest place to begin our investigation of the intensity discrimination mechanism is with the peripheral nervous system. How is intensity coded in first-order fibers? How are changes in intensity reflected in the response of these nerve fibers? There is, of course, a general rule that is true for all modalities. The rule is that increases in stimulus intensity produce increases in the firing rates of the fibers. The earliest recordings from nerve fibers demonstrated this simple fact, and it is widely accepted today as a basic tenet of all sensory physiology. Obviously, subsequent stages of the sensory apparatus may modify and alter the information provided by the periphery, but, at least initially, firing rate increases monotonically with intensity.

A second feature of the peripheral nervous system, appreciated by the earliest investigators, was that the nerve responses showed considerable irregularity. The response of the sensory system, when the input stimulus was fixed, could be more aptly described as some kind of random process rather than a constant response. For example, the total number of neural impulses (spikes) produced by repeated application of the same stimulus varied on repeated applications. One can think of the generation of the spikes as events in a Poisson process. The intensity of the stimulus sets the rate parameter for the Poisson process, but the number of spikes generated on each presentation of the same stimulus varies randomly.

Let us consider how these simple ideas can be used to predict something about the form of intensity discrimination. This general idea was first pursued by McGill and Goldberg (1968a, 1968b). We begin by assuming a unit interval of time, so that the average number of spikes

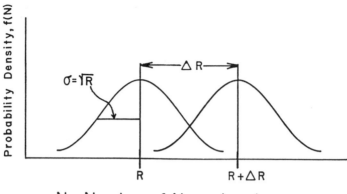

N= Number of Nerve Impulses

Figure 2-1. Probability densities of the number of nerve impulses, *N*, for two different signal levels. The more intense signal increases the number of nerve impulses by an amount, ΔR. The variance of either distribution is equal to its mean. If *R* is large and ΔR small, both distributions have nearly the same variance. For a d' of unity, the increase, ΔR, must be about the square root of *R*. Thus, $d' = (\Delta m/\sigma) = 1 \Rightarrow \Delta R = \sqrt{R}$.

observed during the interval will be equal to the rate parameter of the Poisson process, *R*. If *R* is larger than 20, then the distribution of impulses, contained in our unit count, will be nearly Gaussian with mean, *R*, and standard deviation, $R^{1/2}$. Figure 2-1 shows a distribution of such spike counts, assuming a large number of counts so that the variances of the two distributions are nearly equal. According to this simple Poisson model, a change is detected by increasing the spike count by an amount that is sufficient to overcome its inherent fluctuation. Thus, a noticeable increment in rate, ΔR, will have to be about the size of the standard deviation of the initial distribution, $R^{1/2}$. All of this follows only from the assumption that the spike count is Poisson distributed.

Next we need to consider the relationship between the rate parameter, *R*, and the intensity of the stimulus, *I*. We know they are monotonically related, so let us assume a general functional relationship of that kind and see what predictions can be generated. Specifically, we assume

$$R = f(I) \qquad \text{Eq. 2.1}$$

where *f* is monotonic increasing and smooth enough to have derivatives for all values of *I*. Let us next calculate ΔR,

$$\Delta R = f(I + \Delta I) - f(I) \qquad \text{Eq. 2.2}$$

Note that if we divide both sides of Eq. 2.2 by ΔI, then the right-hand side is, by definition, the derivative of *f*(*I*), as ΔI approaches zero. We can, therefore, rewrite Eq. 2.2 as follows:

$$\Delta R = \Delta I f'(I) \qquad \text{Eq.2.3}$$

where $f'(I)$ is the derivative of $f(I)$. Further, we know that ΔR will be just detectable if it equals the standard deviation of the fluctuation $R^{1/2}$. Hence.

$$\Delta I f'(I) = [f(I)]^{1/2} \qquad \text{Eq. 2.4}$$

Dividing both sides by I, we find

$$\Delta I/I = [f(I)^{1/2}]/[If'(I)] \qquad \text{Eq. 2.5}$$

Only if the right-hand side of Eq. 2.5 is constant will this Poisson model predict Weber's law; namely, that the ratio $\Delta I/I$ is a constant. Let us briefly explore two very popular assumptions concerning the function, f, and see if they are able to predict Weber's law.

The first relationship is the logarithmic one,

$$R = f(I) = a \ln I \qquad \text{Eq. 2.6}$$

In that case, substituting in Eq. 2.5, we find

$$\Delta I/I = (\ln I/a)^{1/2} \qquad \text{Eq. 2.7}$$

and this relationship predicts that the Weber fraction will increase with intensity. No data show such behavior.

A second relationship is to assume a power law, namely,

$$R = f(I) = aI^b \qquad \text{Eq. 2.8}$$

In that case,

$$\Delta I/I = 1/(ba^{1/2} I^{b/2}) \qquad \text{Eq. 2.9}$$

Only if $b/2$, the exponent of I, is near zero will $\Delta I/I$ be nearly constant as a function of I. But, as b approaches zero, then the term $1/b$ predicts that the Weber fraction will be very large. Clearly, there are problems with either of these simple models. In the appendix to this chapter, we derive a function, $f(I)$, that does predict Weber's law, that is, it makes Eq. 2.5 equal a constant. This function, however, is complicated and has no simple interpretation. In sum, there is still no satisfactory explanation of why Weber's law should be approximately correct, given these simple Poisson ideas.[1]

RATE FUNCTIONS AND DYNAMIC RANGE

Although the simplest Poisson view has difficulty, it is not surprising that there is a persistence of the view that intensity discrimination depends in some way on a discrimination of a change in firing rate of some auditory neurons. One reason we are reluctant to abandon this idea is that it is consistent with classical auditory theory. According to the classical view of Ohm and Helmholtz, frequency is coded by place and intensity is coded by firing rate. Another reason for this view is the statistical properties of discharge patterns measured in the auditory fibers. This information emerged from a series of extremely important papers by Kiang (1965) and his collaborators using click stimuli and by Rose and his collaborators using sinusoidal stimuli (Rose, Brugge, Anderson, & Hind, 1967; Rose, Hind, Anderson, & Brugge, 1971). Both sets of investigations showed that there was a strong resemblance between the generation of spikes in the first-order fibers and the assumptions about events in a simple Poisson process. First, as is central to any Poisson process, the occurrence of the next spike appeared to be a random event and nearly independent of the time when the last spike occurred. Second, the data showed that the rate parameter of the Poisson process (the average number of spikes generated per unit time) depended on the intensity of the stimulus. More intense stimuli produce higher rates, and, hence, one may assume that the rate parameter of the process is a monotonic function of stimulus intensity.

There are two complications with this description. First, the nerve fibers have a refractory period of approximately one millisecond that will limit the shortest interval within which another spike can be initiated. Thus, the Poisson process must be modeled as having a deadtime of approximately one millisecond. Teich and Lachs (1979) have provided a detailed analysis of how refractory period influences the data on intensity discrimination. A second complication is that the nerve fires almost exclusively on one polarity of the waveform. The process of exciting a fiber can be modeled as a half-wave rectifier. The fiber can be stimulated only during one half period of a sinusoid; during the other half period, the fiber almost never fires. Thus, the statistical process that most closely mimics the nerve action is a nonstationary Poisson process with an intensity parameter that varies as a function of the amplitude of the pressure waveform and a deadtime of about one millisecond imposed after each spike. A number of recent papers have explored the question of how best to model the statistical properties of auditory nerve processes and have suggested refinements to the earlier, cruder models. The papers by Teich and Lachs (1979), Teich and Khanna (1985), and Young and Barta (1986) are recommended. One should also be aware of the recent progress in attempting to model the discharge patterns as a "point process" (Johnson & Swami, 1983; Jones, Tubis, & Burns, 1985).

This simple statistical view of peripheral processing has great appeal and would still be strongly held as an exclusive explanation of the process of intensity discrimination in the auditory sense if later research had not seriously undermined this notion. The problem is the dynamic range of sounds one can hear compared with the dynamic range of practically any peripheral fiber. We hear, and can discriminate, sounds that vary over a range of 0 to 100 dB, perhaps 0 to 120 dB. Peripheral fibers change their response rates over only a 20- to 30-dB range. Let us call the intensity needed to increase the firing rate noticeably above spontaneous activity the threshold intensity of the fiber. If we increase the intensity about 20 to 30 dB above this threshold intensity, then the fiber will be firing at about its maximum or saturation rate, some 100 to 300 spikes per second. Further increases in intensity will increase this spike rate by very little, if at all.

Saturation then clearly precludes the idea that a single fiber codes the entire rate of audible intensity. Instead, it suggests an alternative idea; namely, that different ranges of intensity are covered by different fibers. The entire population of fibers is presumed to have different, staggered thresholds that span the full range of intensities. Thus, at any given intensity, some fibers would be operating over a nonsaturating range.[2] Once more, one can assume that detection of a change in intensity can be coded as a change in firing rate of these unsaturated fibers. If this is true, however, then different fibers must code changes in intensity over different ranges of intensity. Hence, at least part of the process of detecting a change in intensity must be mediated by noting changes in the place or distribution of activity over a set of fibers. This view, while plausible, violates the strict form of classical theory, because frequency, not intensity, is supposed to be coded by neural activity at different places.

A recent, and most damaging, physiological finding is that the majority of fibers do not have very different absolute thresholds. The first paper on this important topic was by Kiang (1968). He showed auditory nerve thresholds measured for nearly a hundred fibers in a single animal. At any given frequency region, the thresholds for the fibers fell within a narrow range of no more than 20 to 30 dB. The common belief held before this time was simply wrong. Different fibers have very similar, not very different, absolute thresholds. Thus, the idea that the peripheral fibers have staggered thresholds that cover the dynamic range of hearing is in trouble. Given that each fiber had only a small dynamic range, it was unclear what mechanism would support intensity discrimination over the entire range (100 to 120 dB). Liberman (1978) has provided the most recent, and very careful, investigation of this topic.

Liberman's data are unique in that the results were obtained from four cats reared in sound-treated environments to insure that they were never exposed to loud noise. Probably the loudest sounds these cats heard, prior to the start of the experiments when they were six months old, were their own vocalizations. Liberman studied the thresholds of about 250 auditory nerve fibers in each cat and compared the results with a number of normally reared animals.

The first important finding was that the spontaneous firing rates of the fibers fell into distinct groups. Figure 2-2 shows the distribution of spontaneous rates found in the fibers of the three most sensitive cats. As can be seen, there is considerable variability in the spontaneous rate of different auditory fibers. Many fibers show practically no spontaneous activity. There clearly is a group with a spontaneous rate of about 60 spikes

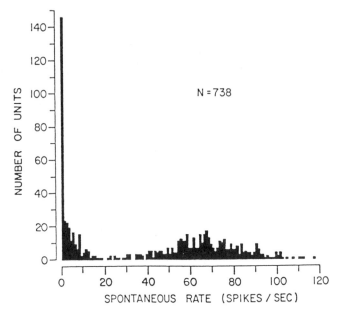

Figure 2-2. Histograms of spontaneous rates sampled from the auditory fibers of three cats raised in specially quiet acoustic environments. The number, N, is the total number of fibers represented in the sample. (From Liberman, 1978.)

per second and another group with much lower spontaneous activity. The group with the slower rates can again be divided into a group showing almost no spontaneous activity and a group with a low, but measurable, spontaneous level. One should appreciate that exploring fibers having very low spontaneous rates is a very difficult experimental problem. Since the physiological condition of the animal can be maintained for only a few hours, it is impractical to obtain detailed data on the fibers with extremely low spontaneous rates. For the present purpose, we will follow Liberman and divide the fibers into three populations. First, there are the fibers with "high" spontaneous rates, 18 spikes per second or more. This group comprises about 61% of the fibers studied. Next, there are the fibers with "medium" spontaneous rates, between 18 and 0.5 spikes per second. This group includes about 23% of the fibers studied. Finally, there are fibers with "low" spontaneous rates, below 0.5 spikes per second. This group comprises about 16% of the fibers studied.

This division of the fiber groups does not appear to depend solely on the animals being raised in special acoustic environments. Liberman found similar patterns of spontaneous activity in his normally raised animals. In addition, Evans and Palmer (1980) found distinct subpopulations in their study of normally reared animals. They state that their fibers "fell into two virtually separate subpopulations . . . with means of

2.3 ± 0.3 S.E. and 55.5 ± 1.6 S.E. spikes/s, respectively." They also agree closely on the percentage of the population in each class, stating that 65% of the fibers had spontaneous discharge rates greater than 15 spikes per second.

In Liberman's 1973 study, the "threshold" for a fiber is computed from an algorithm that presents some tone bursts and adjusts the signal amplitude based on the fiber's response. The signal level at this threshold value in roughly one that increases the firing rate 10 to 20 spikes per second over spontaneous activity, and, according to Liberman, this increase is largely independent of the spontaneous rate of the fiber.

Liberman found that for fibers with high spontaneous activity, those tuned to a common frequency region had thresholds that were virtually identical. The thresholds for fibers with medium and low spontaneous activity were somewhat more scattered. The uniformity of the thresholds for the fibers with high spontaneous discharge rates allows us to use these values as a base line to assess the thresholds for fibers in the other groups.

Such a procedure is used in Figure 2-3, where this relative threshold is plotted as a function of frequency for the "medium" and "low" groups. Some scatter in the threshold values is seen at any given frequency. In addition, the "medium" group is about 10 dB less sensitive than the "high" group, and the "low" group is nearly 20 dB less sensitive than the "high" group. Note, however, that neither group shows a widely scattered range of thresholds compared with the 100–120-dB range of audible intensities. Almost all fibers have thresholds within a range of 30 dB at any given frequency, except for a very few fibers in the two to eight kHz range of the "low" population. Thus, for these noise-protected cats, there is virtually no staggering of thresholds, except in a handful of fibers tuned to the mid-frequency region.

Among a more typical population of animals, the facts will be very similar. Presumably, normally reared animals undergo more acoustic trauma and such trauma appears to lessen the number of fibers with very high spontaneous discharge rates, especially at high frequencies (Liberman, 1978). Thus, in normal animals we find fewer fibers having high spontaneous rates, and, consequently, a more continuous distribution of spontaneous activity. Normal animals, for some reason, show a somewhat wider range of thresholds at any given frequency. But distributions with ranges of 30 to 40 dB are small compared with the 100–120 dB range of intensity discrimination.

A second important aspect of how intensity information is coded in the auditory system is the dynamic range of the fiber. Liberman measured how the firing rate of the fiber changes as a function of intensity. These functions are called "rate" functions, and Liberman's data are sufficiently detailed so that we can look at rate functions for these fibers classified on the basis of spontaneous rate. For the fibers with high and medium spontaneous activity, the maximum firing rate is on average about 200 spikes

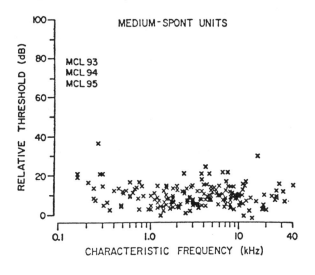

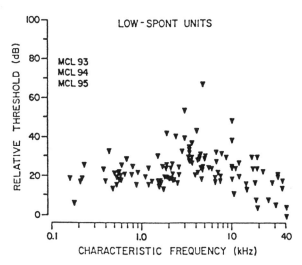

Figure 2-3. The relative threshold of a fiber and its characteristic frequency for fibers with medium and low spontaneous activity. The value for 0 dB on the ordinate is the average threshold for the fibers with high spontaneous activity. (From Liberman, 1978.)

per second and is achieved at a sound pressure level about 30 dB above their absolute threshold. For the fibers with low spontaneous activity, the maximum rate ranges from 20 to 160 spikes per second. This maximum rate is achieved by increasing the intensity of the signal about 20 dB above the fibers' threshold. Obviously, the low and medium fibers show a much larger *relative* change in rate from their spontaneous to their maximum rate than do the fibers with high spontaneous activity.

Evans and Palmer (1980) found a somewhat wider range of values for the dynamic ranges in their population. They discovered that the mean dynamic range was 41 dB for fibers with spontaneous rates above 15 spikes per second and 50 dB for the fibers with the lower spontaneous discharge rates. These differences between the estimates of Liberman and those of Evans and Palmer are difficult to assess, although some may be procedural. Evans and Palmer used much more intense stimuli in their estimates of the rate function than did Liberman. High sound pressure levels were avoided by Liberman to minimize any chance of acoustic trauma, but they may have led to underestimates of the asymptote. Also, there may be differences in the definition of maximum rates. Before the differences in spontaneous activity were fully appreciated, Sachs and Abbas (1974) suggested an equation for the rate function of the fiber in which the threshold of the fiber determines its dynamic range. A fiber with a low threshold would have a dynamic range of about 20 dB; one with a high threshold would have a dynamic range of about 60 dB. Since only fibers with low spontaneous activity have high thresholds (Liberman, 1978), and such fibers, on average, have larger dynamic ranges (Evans & Palmer, 1980), there is some empirical support for Sachs and Abbas's generalization.

In summary, the bulk of the experimental data provides little support for the notion that fibers with staggered thresholds mediate the discrimination of a change in intensity, at least over the entire intensity range. Another type of physiological coding must occur.

FREQUENCY SELECTIVITY

Another aspect of auditory functioning extremely important to the topic of intensity discrimination is frequency selectivity. As Ohm and Helmholtz suggested in their classical theory of hearing, the auditory stimulus first undergoes frequency analysis so that only a restricted band of frequencies stimulates a particular set of auditory fibers. The details of this first stage filtering and how it is observed in both peripheral recording and in psychoacoustic data must be reviewed before we can understand the current functional views of the intensity discrimination process. Indeed, an entirely different approach to the problem of intensity discrimination, usually called "excitation models," is based on the facts of frequency selectivity. This approach suggests another interpretation of the intensity-discrimination process that avoids many of the problems associated with the limited dynamic range of the first-stage fibers (Florentine & Buus, 1981; Whitfield, 1967; Zwicker, 1958).

Frequency selectivity is a pervasive phenomenon in the early stages of auditory processing and is evident in the tuning curves that can be measured in all peripheral auditory fibers. A tuning curve is defined as the locus of all frequency and intensity values that will produce a just-detectable increment in the spontaneous activity of a fiber. At some frequency, the fiber is excited by a minimum amount of energy. This is called the characteristic or best frequency for that fiber. As one changes the frequency of the sinusoid, either above or below this frequency, more and more energy is required to stimulate the fiber. Tuning curves were first measured by Galambos and Davis (1943), and it is now routine to begin practically any study of the auditory periphery by first measuring the fiber's tuning curve. In effect, such a curve reveals where, along the basilar membrane, the fiber is located. There is a tonotopic mapping of frequency and place along the membrane, as demonstrated by a number of studies following von Bekesy's work in the early thirties (von Bekesy, 1960). The maximum place of motion for the high frequencies is located near the stapes, and lower frequencies are located farther down the membrane toward the tip of the cochlear tube.

Figure 2-4 (from Liberman, 1978) shows a number of such tuning curves measured for fibers with high, medium, and low levels of spontaneous activity. The figure demonstrates that the tuning is similar for all types of fibers, independent of their firing rate. The absolute sensitivity of the fibers depends on their spontaneous rates, as we discussed in the preceding section. If the curves are plotted relative to the intensity of the tip, however, as the right side of the figure shows, the different tuning curves are all remarkably similar. Examples are shown for two different frequency regions; in both cases, the tuning curves are nearly identical once the difference in absolute sensitivity had been removed. The tuning may be entirely mechanical, and the result shown in Figure 2-4 would be consistent with such a hypothesis, although other investigators (e.g., Evans, 1974) believe there is some active, physiological process responsible for part of the tuning.

For our purposes, we simply note that a considerable degree of frequency selectivity is evident at the very first stage of auditory processing. Different fibers are tuned to different frequency regions. Each is most sensitive to its own characteristic frequency, and frequencies an octave or so away from that frequency are effective only if the sound is some 40 to 60 dB higher in level.

Such frequency selectivity is also evident in psychoacoustic experiments. One of the earliest studies was that of Wegel and Lane (1924). They studied how one sinusoid, the masker, made another sinusoid, the signal, difficult or impossible to hear. As one might expect, only maskers close to the frequency of the signal influence its threshold. Sinusoidal maskers more remote from the signal frequency can cause masking, but only if we increase their level greatly. Indeed, Wegel and Lane analyzed their data three years prior to von Bekesy's investigations and suggested the degree of filtering or resonance that they believed would be found when the investigation of the basilar membrane mechanics could be carried out.

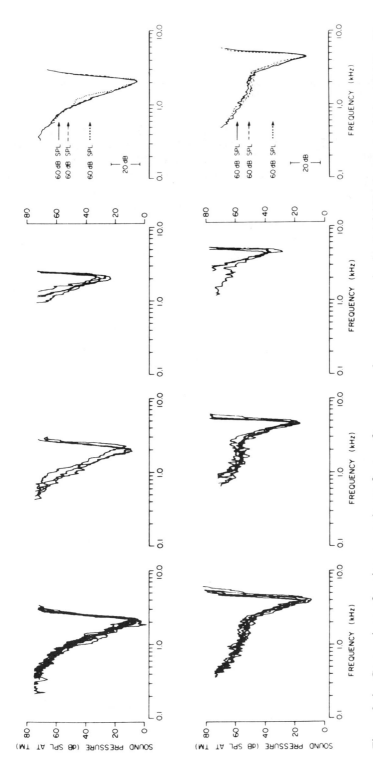

Figure 2-4. Comparison of tuning curve shapes for two frequency regions: upper panels about 1.8 kHz, lower panel about 5 kHz. The panels, from left to right, display tuning curves obtained from fibers with high, medium, and low spontaneous activity. The panel furthest right is a superposition of the individual tuning curves obtained by adjusting the three curves to have a common tip. (From Liberman, 1978.)

Beyond doubt, the most influential experiment demonstrating frequency selectivity was that of Fletcher (1940). He used noise bands of various widths but constant spectrum level and studied how they masked a sinusoidal signal located in the middle of the noise band. Although his data points are not as impressive as his theoretical insight, the results were clear enough. Only a very narrow range of noise components is really effective in masking the sinusoid. For example, at a signal frequency of 1000 Hz, his data showed that only the noise components in a band 60-Hz wide are effective in masking the sinusoid. If the noise band is narrower than 60 Hz, the signal becomes easier to hear. If the noise band is wider than 60 Hz, the threshold of the signal is unaffected. This last finding is counterintuitive, because increasing the bandwidth of the noise increases its loudness, yet the threshold for the signal remains unchanged. Thus, only noise energy in this narrow region about the signal frequency, which Fletcher called the "critical band," is really effective in masking.

Since that time, the critical band has been implicated in a number of psychoacoustic results. There is some difference of opinion as to the exact width of the critical band, but these differences we may regard as details (Scharf, 1970; Patterson, 1974, 1976; Weber, 1978). For our purposes, it is clear that the first stage of auditory processing is a relatively narrow frequency analysis. Only energy in a narrow frequency region produces a measurable change in the output of that filter. Energy outside the critical band is largely ineffective and can be ignored, since it will have little effect on the threshold of a signal located within the band.

TRADITIONAL FUNCTIONAL DESCRIPTION

Although, as we have seen, there is considerable uncertainty about the exact mechanism underlying intensity discrimination, a general consensus still exists about a broad functional description. We will present what we call the traditional view first, and then contrast that view with some of our recent experiments on profile analysis. This description will also enlarge our area of concern. So far, we have devoted our attention exclusively to sensory events. Our sole concern has been how information about intensity is encoded or discriminated within the nervous system. To compare two or more sensations over time, however, some kind of memory or storage of the sensory information is required.

Figure 2-5 shows a block diagram of the traditional view of intensity discrimination. The process starts with frequency analysis that breaks the spectrum into various bands. The output of these bands reflects the acoustic energy in different regions of the spectrum. Intensity discrimination is achieved by noting changes in these levels. Let us consider a very simple case. Two sounds are presented in succession. One is more intense than the other. How would the traditional view describe the pro-

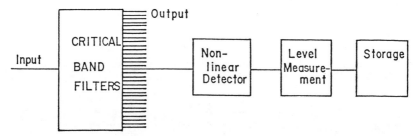

Figure 2-5. A traditional model of auditory intensity discrimination. The acoustic imput is segregated by frequency into different channels. The output of a single channel is then detected and averaged to produce a value roughly proportional to the acoustic level (in dB) for that frequency band. This value is then stored to be compared with another sample taken at a different time.

cess of detecting such a difference? First, both sounds would be filtered so that only those regions of the spectrum in which the intensity might be different would be considered. Next, the level of energy in these regions would be measured for the first and second sound and each would be stored in memory. Finally, a comparison of the two measurements would be made and the one with the greater level would, presumably, be chosen as the more intense sound.

The important feature of this traditional description is the emphasis on the comparison of successive levels over time. Little note is taken of the possibility of simultaneous comparison of different parts of the spectrum during the first or second presentation. This emphasis on successive comparison follows for at least two reasons. First, in most experiments, such as detecting the change in intensity of a single sinusoid, there is only energy in one region of the spectrum. Only a successive comparison can be made because no other energy is simultaneously present to permit such a comparison. Second, even if other energy is present to permit a simultaneous comparison, the critical band experiments show that energy outside the frequency region of the signal does not affect the signal threshold. Thus, simultaneous comparisons are often treated as irrelevant and emphasis is given to successive comparisons.

Although it is seldom discussed, how this process of successive comparison occurs and the memory process used in making the comparison is a very interesting issue. If there is some kind of storage of the first sound's level until the second sound arrives, then the temporal interval between the two sounds should be an important experimental parameter. This interval is seldom systematically manipulated, and its value is largely ignored because, in the range of values typically used, one-half to several seconds, it does not matter. If one uses the conventional experimental conditions, one must use enormous interstimulus intervals to show any effects whatsoever, as Pollack (1955) demonstrated. He presented one of two sinusoidal stimuli to an observer once a day and found a small but statistically significant increase in the Weber fraction—for an interstimulus interval of 24 hours! It is clear from such research that the observers are not noting the level in the first interval and comparing it to the level in the second. Rather, they are comparing the level in the first interval to some long-term standard. The results of this comparison are then stored. This comparison with the long-term standard may then be repeated in the second interval when one must make a decision about the relative level of the two sounds. The interval between the two stimuli is largely irrelevant, however, because the long-term standard provides an easy way to reduce the sensory information to some coded representation that, essentially, does not decay with time.

What we have been describing is what Durlach and Braida (1969) have called "context" coding. They distinguish this mode of processing from a "sensory" coding mode. In the sensory memory mode, the memory is some representation of the sensory event. In the context coding mode, some abstraction of that event is stored. The sensory representation rapidly decays with time; the abstraction does not. The difference is roughly like storing a mental image of a picture—the colors, tone, foreground, background, and perhaps the picture frame—compared with storing a brief description—a picture of a young woman with an enigmatic smile. The sensory image is labile, that is, it is likely to be disrupted by subsequent stimulation. The coded representation is relatively permanent and impervious to interference, but, compared with the sensory store, less detailed or complete.

Tanner was the first to demonstrate that interstimulus intervals of a few seconds could have a noticeable effect when he randomized the level of the standard over trials (Tanner, 1961; Sorkin, 1966). Berliner and Durlach (1973) were the first to systematically employ this procedure to explore the liability of the sensory mode of coding. In their experiments, the observer was trying to detect a difference in intensity between two sinusoidal signals. Instead of fixing the level of the two sinusoids on each trial, as was the usual custom in almost all previous research, the overall level of the two stimuli was randomly varied from trial to trial. Thus, the observer might be asked to discriminate 30 from 31 dB on one trial, and 60 from 61 on the next. Berliner and Durlach used the phrase "roving level" to describe this procedure. Clearly, it is impossible to develop a long-term standard in such an experiment, since the overall level of the stimulus is a random variable. Their results showed a marked deterioration of discrimination performance as the temporal interval between the two sounds to be compared exceeded about one second. Discrimination performance continued to decline out to about 10 sec. Presumably, at very long intervals, the observer would be forced to use context coding rather than a sensory code, but the exact time at which this happens probably varies from task to task and from person to person. We were able to repeat this result of the effect of the interstimulus interval in one of our early experiments on profile analysis, and a description of that result will be the concluding section of this chapter.

PROFILE ANALYSIS

For some time, we have been studying behavior in an intensity discrimination task that appears to be quite different from that explained by the traditional view. A typical task is to detect an increment in the intensity of a single tone of a multitonal complex. From an operational viewpoint, this task is an intensity discrimination study of the Weber fraction for a single sinusoid, except that there are several other tones present in the spectrum. Because these other components are present, a critical feature of this task is that the shape of the spectrum is actually changed when the increment is added to the background or standard spectrum. In almost all traditional experiments of the intensity discrimination process, the spectrum is not changed in shape; rather, it is increased or decreased in overall level. Profile analysis is the term used to describe the mechanism of detecting such a change in spectral shape. For such tasks, we believe a critical feature in the detection process is the *simultaneous* comparison of the energy level in a region of the spectrum where the increment may be present with energy at some other region. We believe that one detects the increment by comparing the levels of different frequency regions at the same time, rather than by comparing the same frequency region at different times. In short, one compares the spectrum level at two different frequencies rather than two different times. Profile analysis emphasizes *simultaneous* comparison while the traditional view emphasizes *successive* comparison.

Accepting the idea of a simultaneous comparison process in these new experiments does not mean that successive comparison is impossible or never used. For those tasks, where the spectrum changes in level and not shape, the older traditional analysis must be used, since only successive comparison is possible. We do believe, however, that the observer can make simultaneous comparisons whenever the spectrum is rich enough to permit such comparisons. Nor is there a paucity of such sounds in ordinary experience. Most sounds contain significant energy distributed throughout the spectrum, such as musical sounds, machinery noise, and speech.

Although we could defend the proposition that behavior in these profile tasks is intensity discrimination, since operationally that is how the stimulus is produced, such changes would not usually be described by listeners as changes in intensity, but as changes in the "quality" of the sound. Perhaps change in "timbre" is the most apt description, although we are reluctant to use that term because there is so little consensus on precisely what it means. An example may make the point clearer and will also suggest another important property of such stimuli. If one hears a clarinet and an oboe playing the same sustained note, then one immediately identifies one of the sounds as a clarinet and the other as an oboe. If asked how the discrimination is accomplished, the listener would undoubtedly use some qualitative terms like the shrillness or brightness of the instruments. In fact, from a physical point of view, the differences between the two sounds could be described as differences in the intensities of the overtones relative to the intensity of the fundamental. With any sound more complex than a single sinusoid, the natural description of the difference between the sounds is a qualitative one, rather than a description of the relative loudness of certain components. Indeed, loudness is not an obvious way to explain such differences, because the overall level of the sound is not a critical variable in a qualitative description of the sound. When describing the difference between a clarinet and an oboe, one usually ignores differences in overall loudness, since this attribute would depend on irrelevant factors such as one's relative distance from the two sources.

In addition to these qualitative descriptions of "profile" stimuli, we believe that they are stored in memory in a manner different from that used to store differences in loudness. These qualitative differences are largely categorical. For profile stimuli, one does not store the relative loudness of an overtone compared to the fundamental. Rather, one remembers its quality, that is, oboe-like or clarinet-like. We will present some empirical evidence to support this speculation in the next section. Let us now turn to the experiment.

EFFECT OF THE INTERSTIMULUS INTERVAL

This experiment studied the memory requirements of several different intensity discrimination tasks. We know, from Berliner and Durlach (1973), that variation in interstimulus interval produces marked changes in detection performance if we use a roving-level procedure. In that procedure, the task is to detect an increment added to a standard that randomly varies in intensity from trial to trial. In a two-alternative forced-choice task, the observer hears, on each trial, two sounds that differ by the increment. The observer cannot adopt a long-term standard, because the intensity varies over trials. This procedure, called *between*-trial variation, should be distinguished from a *within*-trial variation, in which the intensity level of each sound, even on the same trial, is chosen at random.

The experiment consisted of two major conditions and two controls. The first major condition is simply to repeat the single sinusoid condition of Berliner and Durlach. The task is to detect an increment in a 1000-Hz sinusoid with the level of the standard randomized *between* trials. The exact value of the standard was chosen from a uniform distribution of intensities with a range of 40 dB in 1-dB steps. The second major condition is to detect the same increment in a 1000-Hz sinusoid, except that there are 20 other sinusoids present. The other components are all equal in intensity to the standard and all components are equally spaced in logarithmic intervals from 300 to 3000 Hz. We call this a "profile" condition, since the other components provide a background or profile against which the increment in the central component can be judged. The increment is added to the central component of the complex. If the observer makes a simultaneous comparison among the different components of the complex in this condition, then the absolute level of the stimulus should be unimportant. We therefore randomize the overall intensity of the sound *within* trials. Thus, the two sounds to be compared on a single forced-choice trial may differ in overall intensity by as much as 40 dB.

The independent variable for both these conditions is the interstimulus interval, which ranged from one-half to eight seconds. Presumably, if the observers must remember a stimulus trace, as should be the case in the first condition, then that trace should deteriorate over the interstimulus interval. If the sensation stored is some categorical quality, as is claimed in profile analysis, then no deterioration should occur as a function of the interstimulus interval.

Two other conditions served as controls. The first control tested whether there is any difference between increasing the level of one versus 21 components. We want to make sure that any difference between our major conditions is not simply caused by a difference in the number of components that contain the increment. We used the between-trial variation of the first major condition, with a stimulus composed of the 21 sinusoids of the second condition, but, instead of adding the increment to one component of the complex, the same increment was added to all 21 components. This renders simultaneous comparison between components ineffective because there is no change in the shape of the spectrum, only its overall level is altered. Our second control was to run the "profile" condition, the one with a single increment in the central component of the 21-sinusoidal stimuli, using between-trial instead of within-trial variation. Limiting the variation to between trials should make the detection task somewhat simpler because the qualitative comparison can now be made between sounds that are nearly similar in overall loudness.

The results are shown in Figure 2-6. The abscissa is the interstimulus interval in milliseconds. The ordinate is a measure of the size of the increment needed to achieve a certain level of detection performance, about 71% correct in the two-choice task. We will devote more time to an exact description of the ordinate value in the next chapter. For now, it is sufficient to understand that higher values mean poorer detection performance because a larger increment is required to achieve the same percent correct level. The data are average results obtained for three observers, but the individual observers all showed the same trends. The standard error for a single observer for any condition of the experiment is about one to two dB, so differences greater than three dB are certainly reliable.

The results are quite clear. The two conditions in which profile analysis is impossible (namely, as increment in a single sinusoid or an increment in all 21) show progressive deterioration in performance as a function of

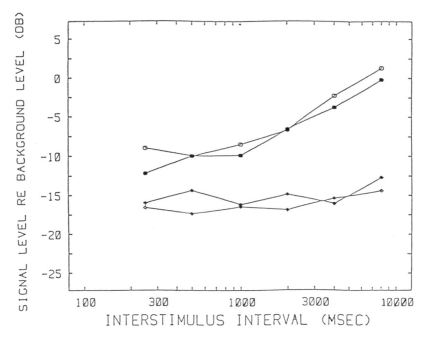

Figure 2-6. The average signal threshold as a function of the interstimulus interval for four stimulus conditions. The two lower curves represent conditions where the signal produces a change in spectral shape. The signal is an increment in the central component of a 21-component standard. The intensity level is randomly varied over a 40-dB range, between trials (open diamonds) or within trials (closed diamonds). For the two upper curves, the signal does not produce a change in spectral shape. One curve displays the data on detecting an increment in a single sinusoid (filled circles) or on detection the same increments in all 21 components of a 21-component standard (open circles). The level of the sound on each presentation varies beween trials over a 40-dB range.

the time between the two sounds to be compared. The other conditions, which allow profile analysis, show essentially no change with interstimulus interval. Thus, our claim that the qualitative differences between "profile" stimuli are largely categorical in nature is supported by these results. Between-trial variation produces marginally better performance than within-trial variation, presumably because the qualitative features are more similar for sounds at similar overall intensity levels.

In the following chapters, we will examine additional evidence supporting our claim of a difference between profile analysis and the other, traditional intensity discrimination tasks. Again, we should emphasize that profile analysis does not replace our traditional view; rather, it points out that discrimination of a change in the shape of spectra may involve quite different processes from those used to detect a change in level over time. Both analyses contribute to our understanding of the intensity discrimination process and will, we hope, aid in our understanding of how intensity information is coded. In the next chapter, we review the data obtained in experiments where the task is to detect a change in the intensity of a single sinusoid.

APPENDIX B
How rate must change with intensity if Weber's law is true for a simple Poisson detector

Another way to use Eq. 2.5 is to derive the function $f(I)$ that will make the intensity Weber fraction constant. Formally, this amounts to setting the left side of Eq. 2.5 equal to a constant, $c,$ and solving the following functional equation.

$$c = [f(I)^{1/2}]/[I f'(I)] \qquad \text{Eq. B.1}$$

It is convenient, and actually suggests the solution, if we rewrite this equation in the following form

$$f'(I)/[f(I)^{1/2}] = 1/(cI) \qquad \text{Eq. B.2}$$

Integrating both sides gives us

$$2[f(I)]^{1/2}] = (1/c)(\ln I + d) \qquad \text{Eq. B.3}$$

where d is the constant of integration. Thus,

$$f(I) = [(1/2c)(\ln I + d)]^2 \qquad \text{Eq. B.4}$$

The solution is a square of a logarithm, which is reasonable, since we found that the logarithm alone caused the Weber fraction to increase with I. The square of the logarithm will increase more rapidly and, hence, lead to better detection. The function is not simple, however, nor can it be derived from more elemental considerations.*

NOTES

1. See Zwislocki and Jordan (1986) for a very recent discussion of this topic—they achieve a nearly constant Weber fraction by assuming that the standard deviation of the internal noise is proportional to the derivative of the loudness function.

2. For a detailed discussion of how many fibers are needed to account for our ability to hear changes in intensity and some experimental evidence, see Viemeister (1982).

Acknowledgment—The preceding derivation was suggested by Dr. T. Hanna.

3

Discrimination of a Change in Intensity Level for Sinusoidal Signals

In this chapter, we will review what we know about the discrimination of a change in the intensity of a sinusoidal signal. Considering all studies of auditory intensity discrimination, this stimulus has received by far the most attention. Part of this popularity is the usual analytic approach common to many parts of science. Since sinusoids are the elements of all complex stimuli, understanding the intensity discrimination process for these elemental stimuli will perhaps enable us to generalize that knowledge to more complex stimuli. Another reason for the popularity of sinusoids is that this stimulus appears to violate Weber's law. The just-discriminable change in a sinusoid is not a constant proportion of the initial pressure level, as Weber's law would have it. Rather, the relative increment diminishes slightly, but reliably, as the initial level increases. Why does this happen and what does it reveal about the discrimination mechanism? This topic is usually summarized as the "near-miss" to Weber's law, and it will occupy a major portion of this chapter. First, we will begin with a brief history and a definition of quantities used to describe the results. Next, we will review the data and explanations offered for the "near-miss." Finally, we will conclude with a review of the Weber fraction measured when the intensity of the sinusoid is very close to absolute threshold. In this region, the Weber fraction, at least as defined in pressure terms, is a nonmonotonic function of the initial pressure. This result, sometimes called negative masking, has only recently been explored, and there is still considerable uncertainty about its origin and explanation.

EARLY STUDIES OF THE WEBER FRACTION FOR SINUSOIDAL SIGNALS

We should realize that studies of intensity discrimination employing auditory stimuli were nearly impossible before the electronic revolution of the early part of this century. An obvious way to vary the intensity of a sound was to vary the distance between the sound source and the listener. This is an awkward experimental manipulation, because changing the position of the source must be carried out without introducing other acoustic cures. Moreover, varying the distance from a source does not change the acoustic intensity in a simple way, except in a free field. To further appreciate the magnitude of this problem and the contribution of modern electronics to this area, one might consult a paper published as part of a Report on the Committee of the American Psychological Association on the Standardizing of Procedures in Experimental Tests. In one of the reports, Pillsbury (1910) reviews the various ways used to alter the acoustic intensity of stimuli. Apparently, a popular method was to drop a hard object onto a sounding device such as a board or tuning fork. The intensity of the sound was altered by varying the distance the object fell. A large part of the Pillsbury review is devoted to an analysis of how the resulting intensity changes as a function of the distance the object is dropped. Pillsbury's final recommendation was that we should abandon this approach and use instead a telephone receiver. By varying the amplitude of alternating current imposed on the receiver, better control of the acoustic intensity could be achieved.

Riesz (1928) at the Bell Telephone Laboratories used the new electronic technology to launch a full-scale investigation of the ability to discriminate changes in the intensity of a sinusoidal signal. Because his data were widely cited, especially in secondary texts, and because almost all subsequent studies have employed a different technique for presenting the stimuli to be discriminated, a brief review of his procedures and results seems in order. In 1928, there was no convenient means of turning the sound on and off quickly—the process we call "gating" the sinusoid. The technology had simply not advanced enough to accomplish gating without generating a number of unwanted transient signals. In the early days of electronics, it was difficult to turn on any signal without generating electronic artifacts associated with the sudden change in the condition of the circuit. Small DC voltages would be produced that were unrelated to the desired change in the amplitude of the sinusoid. These artifacts were audible and made it difficult to determine whether the observer was hearing the change in the amplitude of the sinusoid or the artifacts. Riesz, therefore, used an ingenious, indirect means of varying the amplitude of the sinusoidal signal. He employed two continuous sinusoids of nearly the same frequency but different amplitudes. If the difference in frequency is very small, then, as Rayleigh (1877) derived, resulting sound can be expressed as a single sinusoid slowly fluctuating in amplitude (see also Green, 1976). The rate of fluctuation of this resultant is equal to the difference in frequency of the two original sinusoids. The amplitude of the resultant varies between a maximum and a minimum amplitude whose values are related to the amplitudes of the original sinusoids. The maximum is equal to the sum of the original amplitudes; the minimum is equal to their difference. Riesz instructed his observers to set the amplitudes of one of the sinusoids so that the fluctuations in the sum of the two sinusoids was just audible. From these settings, he could determine the smallest change in intensity that one could reliably detect. Riesz's data showed that the Weber fraction, the increment in sound energy compared with the average energy of the sinusoid, diminished by nearly an order of magnitude as one increased the average level from near threshold to 100 dB above that level. This decrease in the *relative* increment is a clear violation of Weber's law.

Most modern studies of the ability to discriminate a change in the intensity of a sinusoid have used a more direct procedure. They have presented a brief burst of a sinusoidal signal and asked whether the sample was the standard or the standard plus the increment. The results obtained with these gated, or pulsed, sinusoids show less decrease in the Weber fraction with changes in the level of the standard, but a violation of Weber's law is still evident. It now appears that the fluctuation technique used by Riesz leads to somewhat different data from that obtained with pulsed sinusoids (Harris, 1963). Before presenting a summary of these more recent studies, we should first define the various measures used to express these results.

TERMINOLOGY AND DEFINITIONS

Despite what many authors imply, no standard terminology exists concerning the appropriate means to express the Weber fraction in audition. *The* Weber fraction or *the* difference limen is defined differently in different papers. Grantham and Yost (1982) have recently summarized some of the different measures and their interrelationships in a five-page paper in the *Journal of the Accoustical Society of America.* If terminology were standard, such a paper would not be needed.

The nub of the difficulty is twofold. First, the auditory stimulus can be reasonably measured either in terms of amplitude (acoustic pressure) or intensity (acoustic power). The two measures are quadratically related, assuming a constant impedance, that is, the acoustic power is proportional to the acoustic pressure squared. Second, there is a long tradition in auditory research of expressing measurements in logarithmic or decibel terms. This is an understandable practice when the basic quantities can vary over several orders of magnitude, but its application to the Weber fraction, which varies over a single logarithmic unit at most, seems to reflect habit rather than necessity. In any case, different expressions exist, and the serious student of this area must be aware of this situation.

We will first define all the relevant quantities and then develop approximations for their interrelations. These approximations, while not sufficiently accurate for most scientific work, nonetheless illustrate the close affinities of all the suggested measures. The approximations also demonstrate the compressive nature of one of the commonly used quantities. Let us begin by assuming that the stimuli to be discriminated are two sinusoids of different amplitudes. We will use the notation A to represent the amplitude of the standard sinusoid and $A + \Delta A$ to represent the more intense sinusoid. The amplitude, A, is an acoustic pressure and measured in units of force per unit area (e.g., dynes per square centimeter). We use A rather than P to avoid confusion between pressure and power.

We could also describe the two sinusoids in terms of their acoustic power rather than pressure. We use the symbol I to represent this power. The acoustic intensity is equal to the square of the acoustic amplitude divided by the acoustic impedance. We can simplify things somewhat by assuming a nominal one-ohm impedance. In that case, the standard sinusoid has an intensity equal to A^2, and the more intense sinusoid has an intensity equal to $(A + \Delta A)^2$. We denote this increment in intensity, ΔI. The value of this increment in intensity is simply

$$\Delta I = (A + \Delta A)^2 - A^2 = 2A\,\Delta A + \Delta A^2 \qquad \text{Eq. 3.1}$$

The Weber fraction could be defined in various ways. Two obvious candidates are: the ratio of the two pressures, $\Delta A/A$, or the ratio of the two powers, $\Delta I/I$. The latter is more often called the Weber fraction, and we will follow that terminology here. Because ΔA is usually small compared with the value, A, if we divide both sides of Eq. 3.1 by $I = A^2$, we can neglect the term $(\Delta A/A)^2$ and thus have

$$\Delta I/I = 2(\Delta A/A) \qquad \text{Eq. 3.2}$$

Thus, these two definitions of the Weber fraction differ by approximately a factor of 2. Many studies have published their results in terms of the Weber fraction, $(\Delta I/I)$, or its amplitude counterpart, $(\Delta A/A)$, on a logarithmic scale, that is, in decibels. In that case, the natural definitions are $K(I) = 10 \log (\Delta I/I)$ and $K(A) = 20 \log (\Delta A/A)$, and, using the approximation of Eq. 3.2, we find

$$K(I) = 10 \log [2(\Delta A/A)] = 3 \text{ dB} + K(A)/2$$

In addition to these expressions, a decibel expression is often used to express another quantity related to the Weber fraction. For reasons I cannot fathom, it also is called the "Weber fraction" (Grantham & Yost, 1982). It is not, however, simply ten times the logarithm of the Weber fraction; rather, it is the level difference between the two sounds that are just discriminably different. Since this quantity is simply the difference between two levels, we follow Florentine and Buus (1981) and use the symbol ΔL and refer to this quantity as the level difference. Grantham and Yost call this quantity the difference limen or "ΔI in db."

$$\Delta L = 10 \log (I + \Delta I) - 10 \log (I) = 10 \log [(I + \Delta I)/I]$$

The logarithm referred to in this definition is the Briggsian, base 10, logarithm. Again, assuming the term ΔI is small compared with I, we can approximate the level difference, ΔL, as follows:

$$\Delta L = 4.343(\Delta I/I) = 8.686(\Delta A/A) \qquad \text{Eq. 3.3}$$

Thus, for small increments, the level difference or Weber fraction in dB is about five times smaller than the corresponding intensity ratio and nearly an order of magnitude smaller than the corresponding pressure ratio. Note that all of these different definitions are proportional to one another, at least for small increments. There is little to recommend any measure as naturally superior to any other, but the highly compressive nature of the level difference should be noted. Since it is not difficult to measure the Weber fraction, $\Delta I/I$, to within 20%, one should certainly report *two* and possibly *three* significant digits when stating the level difference. Whereas, in most psychoacoustic applications, a difference of one decibel is not considered important, in the case of the level difference a tenth of a decibel may well be. Thus, a level difference, ΔL, of 0.6 dB is probably statistically different from 0.4 dB, but of course the same difference may not be noteworthy at greater signal levels, that is, 2.6 dB may not be different from 2.4 dB.

Finally, as Miller (1947) observed, one can also view the process of *discriminating* between two sinusoids that differ in intensity as a *detection* task. From this point of view, the standard amplitude sinusoid, A, is regarded as a masker, and the increment, ΔA, is regarded as a signal added to the masker. The detection task is to detect the signal added to the masker. In this case, it would be natural to express the ratio, $\Delta A/A$, in decibels and to speak of the signal as so many decibels below the masker. We call this quantity, $\Delta A/A$ in decibels, as the signal to standard ratio in decibels, or simply the signal re standard. In fact, this is often the way the two sinusoids are generated. To produce the more intense sinusoid, most investigators hold the masker at a constant amplitude value and create the signal by attenuating the masker and then adding this attenuated signal, in phase, to the masker. Thus, the attenuated signal value is the quantity directly manipulated in measuring the Weber fraction and is the quantity directly measured in the experiment. Other quantities, such as the Weber fraction or the level difference, are usually calculated from the signal attenuation value re the masker. If more than a few hundred trials are used to estimate the threshold value, then changes of 1 to 2 dB in that attenuation value produce reliable changes in detection performance. In Table 3-1, we list the various quantities we have discussed using one-decibel steps in the signal-to-standard ratio. Figure 3-1 presents four panels to show graphically how each of the four quantities we have discussed, $\Delta A/A$, $\Delta I/I$, $10 \log \Delta I/I$, and the level difference in decibels or ΔI in dB, vary as a function of the signal re standard ratio in decibels. As we have observed previously, there is a near linear relation among these different measures as long as the signal to standard ratio is

Table 3-1. Relationship among Weber measures

Sig re Stan Ratio (dB)	$\Delta A/A$	$\Delta I/I$	10 Log ($\Delta I/I$)	Level Diff in dB
−40	0.010	0.020	−17.0	0.086
−39	0.011	0.023	−16.5	0.097
−38	0.013	0.025	−16.0	0.109
−37	0.014	0.028	−15.5	0.122
−36	0.016	0.032	−15.0	0.137
−35	0.018	0.036	−14.5	0.153
−34	0.020	0.040	−13.9	0.172
−33	0.022	0.045	−13.4	0.192
−32	0.025	0.051	−12.9	0.215
−31	0.028	0.057	−12.4	0.241
−30	0.032	0.064	−11.9	0.270
−29	0.035	0.072	−11.4	0.303
−28	0.040	0.081	−10.9	0.339
−27	0.045	0.091	−10.4	0.380
−26	0.050	0.103	−9.9	0.425
−25	0.056	0.116	−9.4	0.475
−24	0.063	0.130	−8.9	0.531
−23	0.071	0.147	−8.3	0.594
−22	0.079	0.165	−7.8	0.664
−21	0.089	0.186	−7.3	0.742
−20	0.100	0.210	−6.8	0.828
−19	0.112	0.237	−6.3	0.924
−18	0.126	0.268	−5.7	1.030
−17	0.141	0.302	−5.2	1.148
−16	0.158	0.342	−4.7	1.278
−15	0.178	0.387	−4.1	1.422
−14	0.200	0.439	−3.6	1.580
−13	0.224	0.498	−3.0	1.755
−12	0.251	0.565	−2.5	1.946
−11	0.282	0.643	−1.9	2.157
−10	0.316	0.732	−1.4	2.387
−9	0.355	0.836	−0.8	2.638
−8	0.398	0.955	−0.2	2.911
−7	0.447	1.093	0.4	3.207
−6	0.501	1.254	1.0	3.529
−5	0.562	1.441	1.6	3.876
−4	0.631	1.660	2.2	4.249
−3	0.708	1.917	2.8	4.649
−2	0.794	2.220	3.5	5.078
−1	0.891	2.577	4.1	5.535
0	1.000	3.000	4.8	6.021
1	1.122	3.503	5.4	6.525
2	1.259	4.103	6.1	7.078
3	1.413	4.820	6.8	7.649
4	1.585	5.682	7.5	8.249
5	1.778	6.719	8.3	8.876
6	1.995	7.972	9.0	9.529
7	2.239	9.489	9.8	10.207
8	2.512	11.333	10.5	10.911
9	2.818	13.580	11.3	11.638
10	3.162	16.325	12.1	12.387

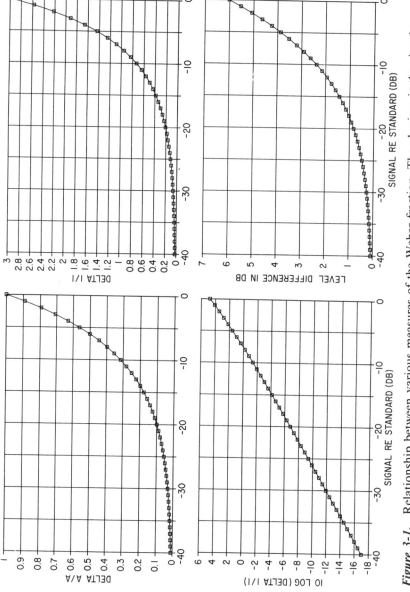

Figure 3-1. Relationship between various measures of the Weber fraction. The abscissa is the signal-to-standard ratio in decibels used throughout. The various other measures are defined in the text.

below about -20 dB. Above that value, these simple linear approximations no longer hold.

As we will see, typical threshold values are -25 to -15 dB in signal to standard ratio. This entire range amounts to a 1-dB change in the level difference, ΔL, again emphasizing the highly compressive nature of that measure. We can now turn to some empirical data. Our first topic concerns the form of the psychometric function. This function relates changes in detection performance to the size of the increment to be detected. This function is important to all empirical studies in this area because it defines the range of stimulus values in the region of the just-discriminable-increment or threshold value. The psychometric function is most conveniently summarized in terms of the signal-to-masker ratio and this reinforces the use of this measure in intensity discrimination tasks.

PSYCHOMETRIC FUNCTIONS

The psychometric function is the function relating some measure of discrimination performance to some physical measure of the stimulus difference. In the case of intensity discrimination, it is convenient to consider a two-alternative forced-choice task. In such a task, we present the standard sinusoid in one temporal interval, and, in the other interval, we present the standard plus increment. If the observer cannot discriminate any difference in the two intervals, then only 50% of the judgments will be correct. As the increment increases in intensity, the detection performance will approach 100%. We will refer to the standard as the masker and the increment as the signal. We wish to know the function that relates the percentage of correct judgments to some measure of the signal. It has been known, since Green and Swets (1966), that this relation has a very simple form if expressed in terms of the detectability index called d'. The psychometric function for an intensity discrimination task is simply

$$d' = c\,\Delta A \qquad\qquad \text{Eq. 3.4}$$

Here ΔA is the increment in pressure or the signal amplitude. The constant, c, depends on the amplitude of the masker, A, the duration of the signal, T, and the acuity of the observer. The measure, d', we have discussed before in connection with Poisson rate model (see Figure 1-1). In the present context, its value can be estimated from the proportion of correct responses in a two-alternative forced-choice task; in this case, it is simply the Gaussian transform corresponding to the proportion of correct responses, that is,

$$\Phi(d'/(2)^{1/2}) = P(c)$$

Where Φ is the area to the left of the unit variance Gaussian distribution and $P(c)$ is the proportion of correct responses in a two-alternative forced-choice task. The $(2)^{1/2}$ arises because there are two intervals, each containing independent samples of the stimulus.

We usually regard a d' value of unity as representing the detection performance at threshold. When $d' = 1$, we denote the signal threshold values as $(\Delta A)^*$. This forces the value of c to be $[(\Delta A)^*]^{-1}$. Thus, if we collect data in a variety of different conditions, we might normalize the data by dividing the measured amplitude ratio by the estimated threshold value $(\Delta A)^*$. In that case, d' should be strictly proportional to the normalized pressure increment.

This procedure was used to construct the data plots shown in Figures 3-2a and 3-2b. The data were obtained in an experiment in which the duration of the signal is varied from 16 to 1000 msec. Data from two observers are shown; they heard two gated sinusoids—one was the masker with amplitude, A, and the other was the masker plus signal with amplitude, $\Delta A + A$. The level of the masker was 60 dB SPL. Two conditions are shown in the figure. In the first, the interval between the two signals (ISI) was 500 msec; in the second condition, the two bursts followed one another with no delay. The purpose of this manipulation was to see if the psychometric function might be altered by some sort of transient events that might be present in the no-delay condition. As you can see, this manipulation seems to have no effect; the psychometric functions appear to be similar.

The form of these psychometric functions is interesting because it is exactly the same form one would expect to see for an optimum receiver. If the receiver were mathematically ideal, or a cross-correlation receiver, then its psychometric function would be given by the following formula:

$$d' = (2E_s/N_0)^{1/2}$$ Eq. 3.5

Here E_s is the signal energy and N_0 is the noise power density to which the signal is added (Peterson, Birdsall, & Fox, 1954). For the ideal receiver, the standard or masker waveform plays no role in the detection task, because it is a constant and could be subtracted from all waveforms. The value of N_0 would presumably represent some internal noise process that limits the receiver's ability to detect the weak signal. If we again assume a nominal 1-ohm impedance, then $(E)^{1/2} = \Delta A$ and Eq. 3.5 is exactly in the form of Eq. 3.4 with the constant, c, equal to $(2/N_0)^{1/2}$. As we have remarked, c should be independent of A for the ideal receiver. The ideal receiver does not follow Weber's law, since only the absolute size of the signal, relative to the noise level, influences detection for this mathematical abstraction.

For the human observer, the value of A definitely does play a role. In fact, to a first approximation, ΔA increases proportionally with increases in A. Thus, to pursue the comparison with the ideal receiver further, one would have to assume that the internal level, $N_0^{1/2}$, must increase proportionally with A so that Weber's law is nearly true. This is obviously an

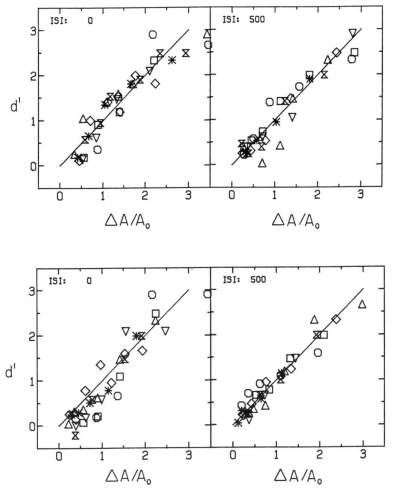

Figure 3-2. Normalized psychometric functions for discrimininating the difference in intensity between two sinusoids for two listeners (*a* and *b*). The data shown represent seven different signal durations ranging from 16 to 1000 msec. The different symbols code the different durations. The abscissa is the increment in pressure for the more intense sinusoid, measured with respect to the pressure difference at threshold ($d' = 1$). The ordinate is the percent correct in a two-alternative forced-choice task converted to d'. The two panels represent different values of the interstimulus interval (ISI), either 0 or 500 msec. The straight line fit shows that d' is proportional to the difference in pressure between the two sinusoids.

unsatisfactory state of affairs, unless one can offer some independent reason for believing that such a relationship should hold.

Before leaving the topic of the psychometric function, we must comment on the variability of our measures, since variability in detection

Table 3-2.   How binomial variability affects threshold estimates

	$d' \pm \sigma$		Signal Level (db)		
n	High	Low	High	Low	Mean/σ
50	1.29	0.74	−17.7	−22.6	3.63
100	1.22	0.80	−18.2	−21.9	4.76
200	1.14	0.86	−18.8	−21.3	7.14
400	1.09	0.90	−19.3	−20.9	10.52

Note: Assume $d' = 1$, (i.e., $p = .76$ and $1 − p = .24$) and that $c = 10$ (i.e., $\Delta A/A = 0.1$).

performance is the source of variability in our estimates of quantities such as the Weber fraction. Ultimately, the variability in our estimates arises because we have to estimate a detection probability, P, with a finite number of observations. This probability, P, should be a fixed quantity, independent from trial to trial if all the physical parameters are held constant. If that ideal situation were the case, then the estimate of this probability should be binomially distributed and have a variance equal to

$$\text{var}(P) = P(1 − P)/n \qquad \text{Eq. 3.6}$$

where n is the number of observations. Since we know the relationship between this probability and d' and because d' is proportional to the signal increment, it is a simple matter to calculate how this variability affects our various measures of intensity discrimination. Table 3-2 shows how these estimates vary for different numbers of observations, n. Thus, the table gives one an impression of the relative variability to be expected in the various measures, although, in this author's experience, binomial variability is generally about 1.5 less than that actually observed in experimental investigations.

In Table 3-2, the high and low values for d' are plus or minus one sigma value from $d' = 1$, assuming binomial variability and the n indicated for that row. The high and low signal level in decibels is computed from the high and low values of d' and Eq. 3.4 assuming that $c = 10$. The mean-to-sigma ratio is computed from the high and low d' values. It increases with n, but only achieves a value greater than 10 for $n = 400$. In that case, the measured threshold value is probably within 10% of the true value. For small signal levels, d', $\Delta A/A$, $\Delta I/I$, and the level difference, ΔL, are all approximately linearly related to each other. Thus, all these measures will have the same relative variability. Using 400 observations or more, we should be able to estimate the signal level corresponding to a $d' = 1$ within 1 dB and should achieve estimates of the Weber fraction within about 10% of the true value.

SUMMARY OF PAST RESEARCH

Previous research in this area has measured the threshold value for the increment in a sinusoid as a function of other stimulus parameters. Given the simple form for the psychometric function (see Eq. 3.4), the summary of past research amounts to specifying how the proportionality constant, c, depends on other experimental parameters. It is convenient to define a threshold value as $d' = 1$, because then the signal increment needed to achieve that value, called ΔA^*, is equal to $1/c$ in Eq. 3.4. Most of our review will focus on how the ratio, $\Delta A^*/A$, changes with various stimulus parameters. The threshold increment is known to change with the level of the standard, A; in fact, this variation has been the main focus of most experimental studies. In addition, the duration of the signal, T, will also influence the threshold, but this parameter has been studied much less thoroughly. The frequency of the signal also has an effect, but only at extreme frequencies. Finally, it appears likely, from the scatter of the mean values estimated in the different experiments, that individual observers vary considerably in their sensitivity. We begin with the question of how the threshold value, ΔA^*, changes with the level of the standard pressure, A.

We are fortunate that Laming (1986) has recently compiled a very detailed summary of the available data. Table 3-3 is adapted from his book. The values listed represent the slopes of least-square regression lines for plots of log $(\Delta A^*/A)$ versus log A. This line estimates the constant, p, in the following approximation to the experimental data.

$$\Delta A^*/A = kA^p \qquad \text{Eq. 3.7}$$

The constant, k, represents the absolute sensitivity of the observer to an increment. It will vary with the sensitivity of the observer, with the

Table 3-3. Near-miss parameter, p, of Eq. 3.7

Harris (1963)	−0.07
McGill and Goldberg (1968a)	−0.14
Jesteadt, Wier, and Green (1977)	−0.14
McGill and Goldberg (1968b)	−0.15
Luce and Green (1974)	−0.15
Dimmick and Olson (1941)	−0.16
Campbell (1966)	−0.20
Campbell and Lasky (1967)	−0.20
Penner, Leshowitz, Cudahy, and Ricard (1974)	−0.20
Viemeister (1972)	−0.22
Schacknow and Raab (1973)	−0.25
Mean ± sigma	−0.18 ± 0.05

Source: Adapted from Laming, 1986.

signal duration, and perhaps with the psychophysical technique used to estimate the threshold value. The majority of the studies listed in the table, however, used the same psychophysical technique, namely, a two-alternative forced-choice task.

If Weber's law were exactly true, then the estimated slope, p, should be zero. The value is clearly not zero but fluctuates about a mean value of -0.18. Thus, if one increases the value of A by 100 dB, then the threshold value of 20 log $(\Delta A^*/A)$ will decrease about 18 dB. This decrease is known as the "near-miss" to Weber's law. It has been confirmed by all studies to date. As noted earlier, this departure is not as great as that measured by Riesz (1928), but a clear departure nonetheless. Later in this chapter, we will summarize various theories that account for this departure. For the present, we will simply summarize the data by the mean value of the parameter, p, namely, -0.18.

One should realize that this slope will be different if the Weber fraction is computed as an intensity ratio. In that case, since $A = I^{(1/2)}$ and $(\Delta I/I) = 2(\Delta A/A)$, we can write Eq. 3.7 as

$$(1/2)(\Delta I/I) = kI^{(p/2)} \qquad \text{Eq. 3.8}$$

Thus, if we plot the data in intensity terms, that is, log $(\Delta I/I)$ versus log I, then the slope of the near-miss is $p/2$, rather than the value of p found in amplitude or pressure coordinates.

Fitting the data by a straight line on logarithmic coordinates is simply a convenient summary of the trend of the data. The major result is that detection of the increment improves, measured in relative terms, as we raise the level of the standard, A. Other summaries have been suggested, most notably Rabinowitz, Lim, Braida, and Durlach (1976). They analyzed over fifteen studies and summarized the data in the following way. For the value of A between 10 and 40 dB SL, Weber's law is true, the ratio $\Delta A/A$ or $\Delta I/I$ is constant. For lower values of A, the Weber fraction increases as A decreases. Above 40 dB SL, the data can be fit by a straight line, such as that of Eq. 3.7, and the value of p is -0.18. Such a summary uses five parameters, two break points, and three slopes. It is, therefore, more complicated than Eq. 3.7. No existing data are sufficiently precise to provide a means of choosing between these two approximations. Our equation provides a simple summary of the previous studies, at least with respect to changes in the level of the standard, A.

Since the standard level, A, does influence the Weber fraction, in order to compare absolute levels of sensitivity among different studies we must normalize the data to a single value, A. Again, we are fortunate because the paper by Rabinowitz et al. (1976) has carried out such a normalization. Table 3-4 is adapted from their paper. Because we are interested in absolute sensitivity, we must use psychophysical procedures that allow us to equate the detectability levels at threshold. All the studies listed in Table 3-4 used a forced-choice procedure so that the threshold value is

Table 3-4. Threshold value of a sinusoidal increment interpolated for a 40 dB
SL standard

Study	Signal Duration (seconds)	20 log $(\Delta A/A)$	Corrected for Duration
Berliner (1973)	0.65	−20.1	−20.1
Berliner and Durlach (1973)	0.8	−20.1	−20.1
Braida and Durlach (1972)	0.5	−19.1	−19.1
Callahan et al. (1973)	0.5	−17.5	−17.5
Campbell (1966)	1.0	−14.2	−14.2
Campbell and Lasky (1967)	0.02	+0.5	−9.2
Haughey (1970)	0.5	−16.5	−16.5
Johnston (1972)	0.5	−18.8	−18.8
Luce and Green (1974)	0.5	−15.0	−15.0
McGill and Goldberg (1968a)	0.02	−10.5	−20.3
McGill and Goldberg (1968b)	0.15	−17.0	−20.6
Penner et al. (1974)	0.1	−11.0	−15.9
Rabinowitz (1970)	0.5	−19.2	−19.2
Schacknow and Raab (1973)	0.25	−17.5	−19.6
Viemeister (1972)	0.16	−17.0	−20.5
Mean over studies ± sigma		−15.5 ± 5.1	−17.7 ± 3.1

Source: Adapted from Rabinowitz, Lim, Braida, and Durlach, 1976.

defined as the signal level when $d' = 1$. We express the threshold value
in terms of $\Delta A^*/A$ in decibels, rather than the sensitivity per bel measure
used by Rabinowitz et al. The value of 40 dB was selected as the nor-
malizing level because it represents a value of A used in nearly all the
studies.

Although the studies listed in the table used a 1000 Hz sinusoid, it does
not appear from other investigations that signal frequency greatly affects
the threshold for an increment, at least if the sensation level of the standard is held constant and the frequency is below 8 kHz. Jesteadt, Wier,
and Green (1977) measured the increment threshold for sinusoids with
frequencies of 200, 400, 600, 800, 1000, 2000, 4000, and 8000 Hz. At
constant sensation levels of the standard, the increment thresholds were
all nearly the same. They used a 500 msec signal duration and varied the
standard level from 5- to 80-dB sensation levels. They summarized their
data with a formula similar to that of Eq. 3.7 with $k = 0.23$ and $p =
-0.14$.

As can be seen in Table 3-4, there is considerable scatter in the estimates from the different studies. The range is more than 20 dB in the
column 20 log $(\Delta A/A)$. It is not entirely clear what is responsible for this
variability. Of course, many differences exist in the procedures used in
the various studies. The interstimulus interval, for one, is different. It
ranges from 200 msec in one study to more than 8000 msec in another.
But a correlation between the logarithm of the interstimulus interval and
the estimated threshold values is nearly zero, so it is not possible to use

differences in this variable to somehow adjust the data. Similarly, some studies used feedback and others did not, but it is impossible to see any clear relation between threshold value and this variable.

One variable that clearly does make a difference is the stimulus duration, which is listed in the second column of Table 3-4. Although this variable has not been extensively studied, we will use the data presented in Figure 3-1 and some published data to develop a scheme to correct the thresholds based on the difference in stimulus duration. In keeping with other data on temporal integration, we will assume that the threshold value improves with a longer duration up to some critical duration and is constant thereafter.[1] The value of the critical duration is typically in the range of 100 to 500 msec. Because so many of the studies in Table 3-4 used a 500 msec duration, we will assume that the threshold does not change beyond that duration. Thus, we need only correct the data of studies that used a stimulus duration less than 500 msec. We used a simple straight-line approximation, plotting the threshold value in decibels versus 10 times the logarithm of the stimulus durations. Calculating such a line from the unnormalized data of our observers shown in Figure 3-2, we found the values for the two observers were: -0.76 for Obs. JS ($r = .97$) and -0.80 for Obs. N.B. ($r = .93$). This means that if we change the duration from 0.05 to 0.5 sec, we should expect the signal-to-standard level to decrease between 7 and 8 dB for these two observers. Garner and Miller (1944) give tabulated data at 1000 Hz, so we can compute corresponding values from their data. The numbers are -0.61 ($r = .97$) for Obs. GAM and -0.62 ($r = .98$) for Obs. WRG. About the only other relevant study is that of Henning (1970), which studied how both frequency and intensity discrimination change as a function of stimulus duration. His data are plotted on a single graph that shows changes in both ΔI and ΔF as a function of duration. On such a graph, the changes in ΔF are much larger than ΔI. It is therefore difficult to read the intensity discrimination data with sufficient accuracy to estimate the slope of the regression line. There is, however, a clear change in the threshold with duration, and it does not appear that Henning's results are very different from our results or those of Garner and Miller. We will use the average value of -0.7 to correct the data of Table 3-4. These corrected values are shown in the last column of the table. As can be seen, the mean of the thresholds, corrected for duration, is then -17.7 dB and the range is reduced to 10 dB.

A simple summary of the data, when approximated in the form of Eq. 3.7, is

$$\Delta A/A = (\tfrac{1}{4})A^{(-1/6)} \qquad \text{Eq. 3.9}$$

This approximation is reasonably accurate if the duration of the stimulus is 500 msec or greater and if the frequency of the signal is in the range 200 to 8000 Hz. This formula predicts that the signal-to-standard level will be -18.7 dB when A is 40 dB SL, -22 dB when A is 60 dB SL, and

−25 dB when A is 80 dB SL. Although (−⅙) is not exactly the average value for the parameter, p, it is the simplest nearby fraction. The value of ¼ is near the mean for the various studies, but apparently considerable variability is present among observers in this value.

The sigma of the mean values of the estimates for the different experiments, even after the effects of differences in duration are made, is still rather large, about 3 to 4 dB (see Table 3-4). That much variability is about three times larger than the variability we expect, if about 400 observations are used to estimate the threshold. Because we have exhausted all the variables known to affect these estimates, this variability must be attributed to differences among the different observers. The general impression in the field is that there is comparatively little difference among observers in an intensity discrimination task. Part of that impression is caused by the very compressive measures often used to express the results of intensity discrimination experiments. It appears that this impression is incorrect; either the observers are very different or there are some very powerful, and as yet undiscovered, factors that influence these experiments.[2]

THEORIES OF THE NEAR-MISS

Two general kinds of theories or explanations have been suggested for the near-miss to Weber's law. The first, suggested by McGill and Goldberg (1968a) in their original publication, is based on the idea that the basic transduction process is nonlinear. This explanation assumes a power law transformation between stimulus intensity and the number of neural counts, n, and uses the simple Poisson model suggested in Chapter 1 as the detection process. To see how such an explanation proceeds, recall that for this model the number of counts, n, is assumed to be Poisson distributed. With the standard sinusoid present, the mean count is n and the standard deviation of that count is $n^{1/2}$. The distribution of counts is nearly Gaussian if n is large ($n > 30$). The signal increment added to the standard will increase the number of counts to $n + \Delta n$. If this increment Δn is equal to the standard deviation $n^{1/2}$, the signal threshold value will be achieved, $d' = 1$. Beginning with the power function,

$$n = kI^a \qquad \text{Eq. 3.10}$$

here k is a constant and a is the power function parameter, presumably $a < 1$, so that n grows less quickly than I. Again, proceeding as in Chapter 1, we find

$$n + \Delta n = k(I + \Delta I)^a \qquad \text{Eq. 3.11}$$

Dividing both sides by n, we have

$$1 + \Delta n/n = (1 + \Delta I/I)^a \approx 1 + a(\Delta I/I) \qquad \text{Eq. 3.12}$$

where the approximation results from using the binomial expansion and neglecting high order terms. Thus, using Eq. 3.10 to substitute for n, Δn can be expressed in terms of I

$$\Delta n = a(\Delta I/I)(kI^a) \qquad \text{Eq. 3.13}$$

Since we want to determine the threshold value of ΔI, or $d' = 1$, we know that $\Delta n = n^{1/2}$ or

$$\Delta n = (kI^a)^{1/2} = a(\Delta I/I)(kI^a) \qquad \text{Eq. 3.14}$$

therefore,

$$\Delta I/I = (1/a)(k^{-(1/2)})I^{-(a/2)} \qquad \text{Eq. 3.15}$$

Thus, the slope of the line relating log $\Delta I/I$ versus log I, the near-miss parameter, is $(a/2)$. In McGill and Goldberg's experiment, that value was about 0.08 or $a = 0.16$. This value for the power function exponent is somewhat disappointing because it is only about half the value of the exponent found in magnitude estimation experiments of loudness. Several investigations have found that direct numerical estimates of the loudness of a sound grow as an approximate power function with an exponent of approximately 0.3 (Stevens, 1975). It would be tempting to believe that the near-miss to Weber's law and direct loudness estimates are both related to one basic fact: the compressive transformation of acoustic energy into neural counts.[3]

The McGill-Goldberg hypothesis attracted considerable attention. Although no direct experimental contradiction of this theory exists, later studies have found that the near-miss parameter changes with certain experimental manipulations. These changes are not explained or predicted by the McGill-Goldberg theory. To review these new experimental findings, we must turn to a quite different account of the near-miss data.

A second theoretical idea used to explain the near-miss to Weber's law assumes that nonlinear changes in the frequency analysis process are responsible for the gradual decrease in the Weber fraction with larger values of I. This explanation begins with the usual place theory assumption that sinusoidal frequency is coded as a place along the basilar membrane. Next, consider the relation between the intensity of a single sinusoid and the locus of stimulation. The sinusoid stimulates not merely a single point along the basilar membrane, but a range of places, depending on the intensity of the sinusoid. To see how this range of places (frequencies) changes with intensity, look again at Figure 2-4. This figure shows how an entire range of tonal frequencies stimulates a single place as we increase the intensity of the sinusoidal stimulus. Now consider the implications of this graph for the stimulation of different places as we change the intensity of a single sinusoid. While a weak sinusoid will stimulate only a very narrow patch along the basilar membrane, a more intense sinusoid will stimulate a wider patch. Since the auditory system is a spatial one, with frequency translated into place along the basilar membrane, this means that as the intensity of the sinusoid increases, a larger and larger area along the basilar membrane will be stimulated.

An implication of this view, coupled with the limited dynamic range of single fibers, is that changes in intensity are coded, in part, by changes in the nerve fibers stimulated. Such an idea is heretical in classical place theory, since classical theory assumes that only place codes frequency and that changes in the total rate codes intensity. But, clearly, the code is somewhat more complicated than the classical theory would have it. In any case, as the sinusoid increases in intensity, more and more fibers, adjacent to the original site of stimulation, respond to the sinusoid. These patterns of neural activity, a joint function of place and intensity, are called "excitation pattern models" (Florentine & Buss, 1981; Whitfield, 1967; Zwicker, 1958). Now, suppose that there is some slight nonlinearity either in the way the acoustic energy is delivered to these remote sites of excitation or in how these patterns evolve as the intensity of the sinusoid increases. A slight nonlinearity in either process may imply that the Weber fraction will not stay constant, but may actually decrease with intensity. To see how this might happen, we first consider the theory proposed by Viemeister (1972).

Viemeister begins with the very reasonable assertion that there must be a measurable amount of harmonic distortion in the ear, and that distortion components will become audible as we raise the intensity of a single sinusoid. Thus, as a sinusoid is increased in intensity, more harmonics of that tone become evident. If these harmonics are generated by a simple kind of nonlinearity, then the amplitudes of the harmonics grow more quickly than the amplitude of the fundamental. For example, if the second harmonic is caused by a simple quadratic distortion, then a 1-dB increase in the fundamental causes a 2-dB increase in the second harmonic. Similarly, cubic distortion that produces a third harmonic would grow at the rate of 3 dB for each 1-dB increase at the fundamental. When possible, the observer is assumed to take advantage of this nonlinear growth at the higher harmonics. For example, if the second harmonic is audible, then a change in intensity at this frequency is twice as great as the change at the fundamental frequency. For small values of A, only the fundamental of the sinusoid is audible and we expect a constant value of $\Delta A/A$. As A increases, the second harmonic becomes audible; thus $\Delta A/A$ would decrease to a value approximately half of the original one. As A increases further, the third harmonic becomes audible, and $\Delta A/A$ would drop to one-third its original value. A plot of $\log \Delta A/A$ versus $\log A$ would resemble a staircase, a series of flat portions with decreases to the next flat portion as A is increased. If one judiciously arranges these steps along A, then one could approximate the function depicting our near-miss to Weber's law quite accurately. These values of A, where the steps must occur, are close to values where other data suggest that the second, third, and higher harmonics of the sinusoid become audible. Thus, there is some independent evidence to lend support to this theory. Indeed, this fact suggests another test of the theory. It is known that there are sizable individual differences in observers' data on the amount and extent of nonlinear amplitude growth. Potentially, one might find sizable differences in the shapes of the near-miss graph for different observers, depending on where the distortion products become evident for the different observers. Such research has not been carried out.

The excitation model explanation is similar in spirit to Viemeister's hypothesis, but less definite about the nonlinear process responsible for the change in the Weber fraction. This theory simply notes that as one raises the intensity of a sinusoid, the form of the excitation pattern does not merely increase proportionately but rather changes its shape. Consider the function showing how one sinusoid masks another. The amount and extent of the masking changes rather dramatically as the intensity of the masker is increased. If the masking pattern changes shape, then the change in the pattern at some place, or frequency, must be different from another place or frequency. The observer can then use the place of excitation where the maximum change in the pattern is occurring to detect the change in the intensity of the increment in the sinusoid. The fundamental idea is very similar to the essential assumption of Viemeister's theory; namely, that as intensity is increased, the just-detectable change will decrease, because the excitation pattern will change more rapidly at some remote place than it does at a place associated with the frequency of the signal.

Both excitation pattern theory and Viemeister's theory would predict that, if one could somehow prevent the observer from attending to these places remote from the signal frequencies, the near-miss should disappear. In short, Weber's law might be correct, if one can restrict the observer to the single frequency channel associated with the signal frequency and avoid the complications in the frequency analysis process that allow these nonlinearities to be manifest.

A simple way to achieve this restriction is to present the sinusoidal signal in the middle of a notched-noise background. In this situation, the observer is forced to listen to change only at the signal frequency. Places of stimulation not near the frequency of the signal are masked by the noise. In such experiments, the data fall very close to Weber's law (Moore & Raab, 1974; Viemeister, 1972). Viemeister's ideas, however, have not received experimental support, since Moore and Raab (1975) did not find the near-miss eliminated with noise placed only above the frequency of the signal. Such noise should obscure the harmonics of the signal and hence make Weber's law true. Similarly, Penner, Leshowitz, Cudahy, and Ricard (1974) and Florentine (1983) measured the Weber fraction of a very high frequency sinusoid. Presumably, the harmonics of such a signal are inaudible, but the near-miss was still evident. We should note that in Florentine's study the high-frequency sinusoid was 14,000 Hz and the near-miss was much smaller at this high frequency than at the lower frequencies she studied. Thus, the most cautious summary of the experimental data is to say that Weber's law will be true only if the sinusoid is presented in a notched-noise background. Such a masker effectively elim- inates listening at all places but those associated with the signal fre- quency. This fact is not explained if one assumes an inherently nonlinear transduction process, such as that suggested by McGill and Goldberg (1968a, 1968b). Thus, the bulk of the evidence favors some sort of non- linearity in the frequency analysis process. If the observer is forced to listen to a single frequency channel, then Weber's law will hold. Finally, we should observe that, although these excitation pattern theories give us an excuse or reason for expecting the near-miss to Weber's law, they do not explain why Weber's law is true for a single channel.

WEBER'S LAW NEAR ABSOLUTE THRESHOLD

So far we have discussed the detection of a change in intensity of a sinus- oid at standard intensities from 20- to 100-dB sensation level. Although a few measurements have been made when the intensity of the sinusoid is very low, they are the exception, not the rule. Laming (1986), in his recent book, presents a complete theory of intensity discrimination for a sinusoidal signal at all intensity levels, including the region near thresh- old (see also Laming, 1985). His theory predicts that the just-noticeable change in the sinusoid will be a nonmonotonic function of the standard level when measured as ΔA, or as signal level re standard, and will show a minimum value some 10 to 15 dB above the absolute threshold for the sinusoid. This theory is interesting, because it suggests that a fixed signal increment may become easier to hear as we increase the level of the stan- dard. If we regard the standard as a masker, it suggests that "negative" masking is occurring. Alternatively, we can argue that ΔA is an incorrect measure of the change in the sinusoidal signal. After all, when we add ΔA to A we increase the intensity of the stimulus by an amount $\Delta I = 2A \Delta A + (\Delta A)^2$ (Eq. 3.1). Perhaps this quantity would increase monoton- ically with increases in A. In that case, we could argue that ΔI should be used as our measure of the stimulus. Even if this latter measure is correct, it suggests that understanding this area will provide a "proper" definition of the stimulus and such a definition is certainly a worthwhile goal. Indeed, some have argued that it is the ultimate goal of all psychophysics. While we will probably not be able to settle arguments about the "proper" definition of the signal with any single experiment, or with several exper- iments in a single situation; nonetheless, we should understand the value of the Weber fraction over the entire stimulus range, both large and small. For these reasons, we will review Laming's theory and the limited exper- imental data available on this interesting topic.

Laming's theory assumes that, although the primary receptor elements increase their output as stimulus intensity is raised, these outputs are bal- anced at higher centers with inhibitory outputs of roughly equal and opposite sign. The net result of this near counterbalance of excitatory and inhibitory processes is that changes in the variance of the neural activity, rather than changes in the mean, are the important measures at higher centers of the nervous system. Detecting a change in intensity amounts to detecting a change in the standard deviation or variance of the Poisson process. The mean value of the neural activity is nearly always the same, except for transient events at the onset and offset of the stimulus. Laming assumes these primary elements give a response that is essentially that of a half-wave rectifier. Given this assumption, and some other plausible ones, he derives that the output of this device behaves in two different ways, depending on the amplitude of the input. The output is proportional to the amplitude of the sinusoid at high input levels. At low levels, the output is proportional to the *square* of the amplitude.

At high intensity levels, the change in intensity is reflected by a change in variability. This variability will then be chi-square distributed. This statistic is sensitive only to *relative change.* Thus, the theory explains that Weber's law is true because it asserts that detection occurs for a constant relative change in the stimulus. At low intensity levels, where the change in the output is roughly proportional to the amplitude squared of the stimulus, some unexpected results occur.

The argument is deceptive in its simplicity. At very low levels of stimulation, detection is limited by the inherent noise of the process rather than any factors related to the magnitude of the stimulus. Indeed, at the lowest levels, no signal is audible because it produces a level of activity less than the level of activity inherent in the process itself. A sinusoid first is audible (absolute threshold) when its level is roughly the size of the inherent noise background; let us call this absolute threshold level A_0^2.

Now, suppose we add an increment to that sinusoid. The increment we produce is the square of the input pressures, by assumption, and—to be detectable—that increment will have to be about the size of the inherent fluctuation, which we know from the absolute threshold value to be A_0^2. Thus, the size of a just-detectable increment, near absolute threshold, is about

$$(\Delta A + A)^2 - A^2 = 2A\,\Delta A + (\Delta A)^2 = A_0^2 \qquad \text{Eq. 3.16}$$

If ΔA is small enough compared with A, we can neglect the term $(\Delta A)^2$, and can rewrite Eq. 3.16 as

$$2A\,\Delta A = A_0^2 \qquad \text{Eq. 3.17}$$

where A_0^2 is a constant.

If ΔA is small compared with A, then ΔA varies inversely with A, that is, ΔA actually decreases as A increases. This is negative masking, since the signal level decreases as the masker level increases.

The exact mathematical derivations are considerably more complicated and, unfortunately, no very simple equations have yet been derived

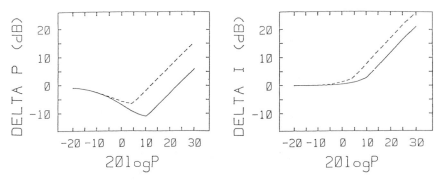

Figure 3-3. Predictions of Laming's theory as to how the threshold for discriminating an increase in level should vary as a function of level of the standard. The standard level is plotted along the abscissa; the ordinate is the threshold value, plotted either as the change in pressure, left panel, or the change in intensity, right panel. The threshold value is predicted to be the value indicated by the dotted or solid line, whichever is greater.

to express the results. The conclusions, however, are in agreement with the simple argument we have just presented. Figure 3-3 shows the two approximation lines that express Laming's theory. The Weber fraction, $\Delta A/A$, is plotted in the left side of the figure; the Weber fraction, $\Delta I/I$, is plotted to the right. The observed data are assumed to fall on the higher of the dotted and solid lines indicated on each graph. Note that, according to this theory, there in no nonmonotonic behavior in the function if intensity, I, is used as the dependent variable. Only if pressure is used will the nonmonotonic nature of the data be evident. Using the pressure scale, the value of the standard, at which the minimum pressure value should be observed, is about 5 dB above the absolute threshold value for the sinusoid. The theory predicts both the form of the function and the value of the minimum and, hence, should be particularly vulnerable to experimental tests. Unfortunately, the available data are slight, and only one study has been carried out since this theory has been presented. Let us now review that evidence.

Figure 3-4 shows a summary of some measurements made by Viemeister (1984). Data from six observers are shown on the graph. The ordinate of the graph is normalized to each observer in that it is the level of the standard sinusoid plotted with respect to the observer's absolute threshold, A_0. Thus, zero on the abscissa is a sensation level of zero decibels for that observer. Similarly, the level of the signal added to the standard is also scaled to the absolute threshold. As can be seen, there is considerable scatter among the observers. Some of this scatter arises because both the abscissa and ordinate have been adjusted by the observer's absolute threshold, which is subject to some error. Nevertheless, it is clear that for these low values of the standard, the just-detectable signal is smaller

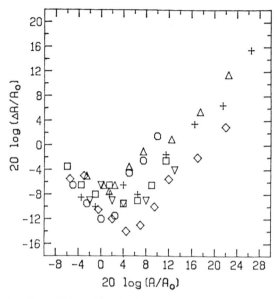

Figure 3-4. Data from Viemeister (1984) showing the threshold for an increase in the intensity of a sinusoid for individual listeners. The level of the standard re the absolute threshold for that listener is plotted along the abscissa. The threshold is plotted as the increase in pressure also re the absolute threshold. Data from six different listeners are displayed. Note the minimum value for the threshold occurs about 4 or 5 dB above the absolute threshold level.

than the pressure level at absolute threshold. Greenwood, in some yet unpublished data, has also measured the increment threshold for a number of observers at very low sensation levels. He also finds a region of "negative masking" when one plots the data in terms of increment pressure.

Stimulated by these measurements, we have recently completed some experiments on this question in our laboratory. The data are presented in a paper by Hanna, von Gierke, and Green (1986). Figure 3-5a and 3-5b shows some of that data. A region of negative masking is clearly

Figure 3-5. The axes are similar to those shown in Figure 3-4. (The data are from Hanna, von Gierke, & Green, 1986.) The two panels show the threshold expressed either as an increase in pressure (top panel) or an increase in intensity (bottom panel). The data were obtained in two listening conditions. In the first condition, the observer listened in quiet, in which case the value of A_0 refers to the absolute threshold value, and the threshold value is indicated on the left side of the figure. In the second condition, the observer listened with a continuous background noise present, in which case the value of A_0 refers to the masked threshold value, and the threshold value is indicated on the right side.

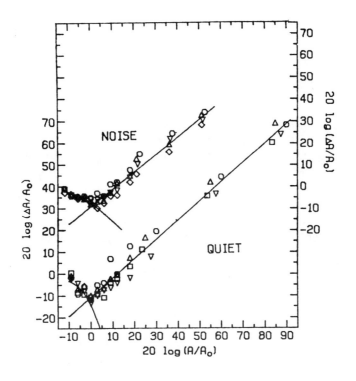

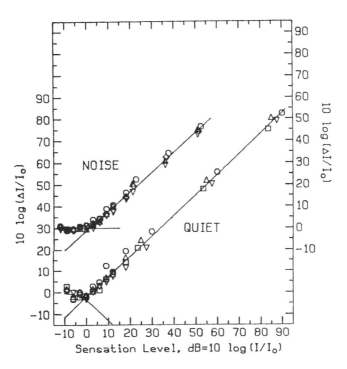

apparent when the data are plotted in pressure terms; it is also evident when plotted in terms of intensity. Thus, it appears that another facet of pure tone intensity discrimination is the a small region of "negative" masking.

SUMMARY

This chapter has reviewed the empirical data relevant to the auditory detection of increments in single sinusoidal signals. First, the terminology has been described. Next, the near-miss to Weber's Law has been discussed and a simple approximation formula that is reasonably accurate in summarizing most of the experimental data has been suggested. It is apparent that there is considerable variability in the absolute level of detection performance measured in the various studies. Whether these differences are caused by differences among subjects or other procedural details is not known. Finally, theories of why the near-miss occurs have been discussed. All agree that some kind of nonlinear mechanism in the growth of stimulation with level is the most probable reason for the departure from Weber's law. Recent experimental data taken in the intensity region near absolute threshold reveal a small region of negative masking. This data can be accounted for by another nonlinear theory suggested by Laming.

NOTES

1. A recent article by Florentine (1986) has provided detailed data on the topic of time-intensity trades for pure tone intensity discrimination. She found the critical duration much longer than those in threshold measurements, especially at the higher frequencies. At 1000 and 2000 Hz, the critical duration appears to be in the 1- to 2-sec range. Her data on the improvement in threshold with signal duration are in rough agreement with the approximation developed in this chapter, particularly over the range of durations found in Table 3-4.

2. A recent paper has presented data on the level difference, ΔL, for ten observers (Zwicker & Henning, 1985). The signal was a 250-Hz sinusoid. The authors state that "individual differences in listeners with normal hearing rarely exceed a factor of two" (p. 31). In fact, as Figure 2 of their paper demonstrates, the range, from less sensitive to most sensitive listener, is nearly a factor of 6 at 50 dB and a factor of 3 at 70 dB. A range from 0.5 to 2.0 in ΔL corresponds to a change of about 12 dB in terms of signal-to-standard ratio.

3. See Zwislocki and Jordan (1986) for a more recent and more extensive discussion of this issue. They propose that the internal noise is proportional to the derivative of the loudness function.

4

Some Properties
of Profile Analysis

In the previous chapters, we have made the case for describing the detection process, at least in some experiments, as a simultaneous comparison of different regions of the spectrum. We call this process by the shorthand name of profile analysis. We have contrasted this simultaneous mode of processing to that of successive comparison in which the observer compares the sound levels in a particular spectral region measured at two different times. To encourage the simultaneous mode of processing, we often randomize the overall level of the sound presentation. In that way, successive comparisons are largely ineffective, since comparisons of different presentation levels provide little information about the presence or absence of the signal. In this chapter, we review some experiments that illuminate some properties of this profile analysis process. Although some of these properties resemble those studied in the more traditional experiments, where successive comparisons are common, many of the properties are different.

IS PHASE IMPORTANT?

We begin with an experiment on the effect of phase because understanding the role of this variable is crucial to understanding the best way to define the stimulus. As we will see, phase has essentially no effect. Thus, only the distribution of energy over frequency, that is, the power spectrum, is critical in describing the stimulus. This simplification is our first insight into at least one property of the profile analysis process. The experiment that demonstrates the irrelevance of phase is as follows.

In many profile analysis experiments, the background or standard stimulus is a complex of several equal amplitude sinusoids. Typically, the components are equally spaced on a logarithmic frequency scale (i.e., the ratio between successive frequency components is a constant). The phase of each component of the multitonal standard is selected at random and, once the standard is digitally generated, it is stored and used for a number of experimental trials. Thus, the standard has the same waveshape on each and every presentation. It is conceivable that the auditory system could somehow learn this standard waveform and detect the signal by noting a change in this waveshape. Such a hypothesis may appear to be farfetched, especially because, following Helmholtz and Ohm, many of us believe the power spectrum of the stimulus is the best basic description of the stimulus and that phase is relatively unimportant. But, detection of the signal by noting a change in the standard waveform is one conceivable detection strategy, and this hypothesis should be rejected on the basis of empirical results, not theoretical bias.

To explore this hypothesis, the following experiment was conducted (Green & Mason, 1985). First, we generated a number of different waveshapes for the multitonal standards. The standards were composed of either 5, 11, 21, or 43 components. For each number of components, four different waveshapes were constructed by selecting different phase randomizations for the components of the multitonal standards. The threshold for a sinusoidal signal, added in phase to the center component of the complex, was then determined for each of these four standards. If the signal is detected by noting a change in the waveshape of the standard, then one might expect that the signal threshold might change depending on which standard waveshape we used, that is, the signal threshold might vary as we vary the phase relations among the components. The results did not support this hypothesis; see the four open points plotted for the different number of components in Figure 4-1. This is Figure 3 of the original article of Green and Mason (1985). The scatter of thresholds among the four different waveshapes is not appreciably greater than the error of measurement usually encountered in measuring the threshold of the signal on repeated determinations with the same standard. This experiment is far from crucial, however, since it is possible that all four phase randomizations happened to produce four standard waveshapes that were of equal difficulty. More critical is the following result.

Central to the hypothesis that phase—and hence standard wave shape—is an important variable is the claim that the observer somehow learns the standard waveshape and detects the signal by noting an alteration in this learned waveshape. Suppose, however, that we change the standard waveshape on each and every presentation. We accomplish this by constructing hundreds of different standards using a random selection of phase for each component of the complex. For each presentation, we select a standard by drawing at random from this large set of standard waveforms. The waveshape on each presentation will, therefore, be different on each presentation, and it would be impossible to learn the standard waveshape, because it is never the same. It is also impossible for the observer to detect the signal as an alteration in the standard waveform. Thus, if phase were important, then the signal threshold should be much larger for this condition than for the conditions where the same standard

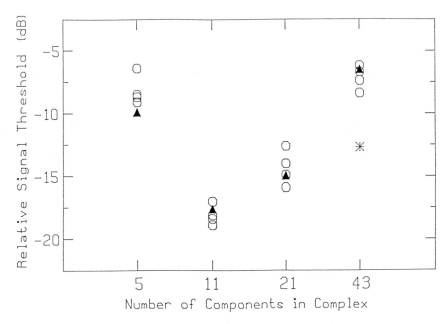

Figure 4-1. Average signal threshold of three listeners as a function of the number of components in the standard complex. The signal is always an increment in the middle component (1000 Hz) of the complex. Open circles represent four different phase randomizations for conditions in which the phase was fixed throughout a block of trials. Filled circles represent conditions in which the phase of the individual components of the complex were randomly chosen on each presentation. The asterisk is a fixed-phase condition in which the six components nearest the signal frequency were removed to lessen the effects of direct masking.

waveform is used on all presentations and the observer can, conceivably, learn the standard waveform. The results indicate that the signal threshold for this random standard condition is not very different from the threshold obtained with the four different standards that were presented on each and every trial; see the solid points in Figure 4-1. It is true whether we use 5, 11, 21, or 43 components in the masking stimulus. In fact, the measured threshold for the 5-component condition in which the standard waveshape changed on each presentation was about 1.5 dB superior to the average of the four thresholds for the condition in which the standard waveform was fixed. For the other conditions, the changing standard condition was near the mean threshold for the four fixed-standard conditions.

We postpone discussion of the point, plotted as an asterisk, about 5 dB below the other points for the 43-component complex. The experimental manipulation for that point involved more than a change in phase among the components and can most easily be discussed after we have concluded the discussion of phase.

This result of the phase manipulations clearly demonstrates that waveshape is not critical, since the threshold for the signal is similar in all these conditions. What is constant is the power spectrum of the stimulus, that is, the magnitude of each component independent of its phase relationship to any other component of the complex. In the remainder of this monograph, therefore, we will describe the background or standard stimulus only in terms of its power spectrum and ignore those variables that do not alter this power spectrum. Given this result, we believe the signal is detected as an alteration in the power spectrum of the standard, not an alteration in the standard waveform. The "profile" against which a change is noted is the power spectrum of the standard.

Finally, we return to the solitary point plotted for the 43-component complex in Figure 4-1. For this point, the power spectrum of the stimulus was altered by canceling six of the components nearest the signal component, that is, we removed three components on each side of the 1000-Hz component. We made this measurement to illustrate that part of the threshold increase caused by increasing the number of components in the masker occurs because of increased masking at the signal frequency. Most of this masking can be attributed to components near the signal frequency. As can be seen, removing some of these components improves the signal threshold by about 5 dB. This explanation, however, does not provide a complete answer to the change in signal threshold with increased density of the profile. With the six components missing, the spacing of the components near the signal frequency is the same as with the 11-component complex. The two components nearest the signal frequency are 734 and 1358 Hz. Despite this similarity, the threshold is about 5 dB higher than that obtained with the same local spacing in the 11-component complex. Consideration of the exact spacing of components in the complex leads us naturally to the next section of this chapter; namely, what profile for the standard spectrum will allow us to detect the smallest relative increment?

WHAT IS THE BEST STANDARD PROFILE?

In essence, the objective of this search is to find a background or standard stimulus that will permit the observer to detect the smallest relative change. We could describe the stimulus to which the observer is maximally sensitive as the optimal profile or standard. To determine such a stimulus, one must either systematically test all possible stimuli or have some reasonably comprehensive theory that suggests the correct answer. Obviously, we have not yet had time to test a very extensive set of standard waveforms and our theoretical understanding of profile analysis is still primitive. Our search is still, therefore, largely empirical, but it is also governed by some theoretical principles that guide our selection of standard stimuli.

For the sake of concreteness, let us assume the signal is a sinusoid and its frequency is in the region of 1000 Hz and the overall level is about 40 dB SPL. Other signal frequencies and levels would change some of the absolute levels quoted in this discussion, but the relative relationships would remain the same. Let us begin by considering the detection of a change in a broadband spectra, such as a sinusoid added to a noise. The detection of such a signal occurs when the signal energy is about 10 dB greater than the noise power density, and the ratio is smallest when the signal durations are between 10 to 100 msec. Let us fix the signal duration at 100 msec, since this value is often used. For this signal duration, the power of the signal re the power in a 1-Hz noise band is 100. The fluctuation of the noise over successive presentations plays a small role because when we use a constant noise waveform on each presentation (so-called frozen noise) the signal threshold is only about 3 dB better, that is, a power ratio of 50 instead of 100. If we assume, for simplicity, that the critical band is about 100 Hz wide at a center frequency of 1000 Hz, then the power in the critical band is 100 times greater. The signal produces a relatively large increment in this band, a 3-dB increment if the signal power is 100 times the noise density and a 1.7-dB increment if the signal power is 50 times the noise density. Note that, in this case, the signal and noise are incoherent, so one simply adds the signal and noise power to calculate the increment.

Next, we might consider a very narrow spectral background rather than the broad continuous background we have just discussed. A logical extreme on this continuum of broad and narrow spectra is a single sinusoidal component with the signal being an increment in its power. In successive presentations of a sinusoid, one can detect an increment in a single sinusoid of about 40 dB at a relative level of -18 dB. (See the review given in Table 3-4.) Thus, a relative power increment of about 25% can be detected, that is, a change in level of only about 1.0 dB. (See Table 3.1.) The increment in the sinusoid is detected at smaller relative levels than those associated with a broadband stimulus. Because of the near-miss to Weber's law, it should be noted that the detection levels for the sinusoidal increment will decrease if we assume that the standard level is greater than 40 dB. In contrast, the threshold for a sinusoid in noise is relatively independent of overall level. We conclude that better detection of an increment in the spectrum occurs if we use a narrow spectral standard rather than a continuous broad spectrum such as that represented by noise. But the detection of an increment in such a narrow spectral stimulus can hardly be based on simultaneous comparisons of different spectral regions because there is no change in shape of such narrow spectra. Since simultaneous comparisons of different spectral levels cannot be carried out with a single sinusoid as the standard, we must add some energy at a different region of the spectrum to provide the basis of profile analysis.

We know some general rules that would govern the best place to distribute this energy in the spectrum. Suppose the signal is an increment in the 1000-Hz component and we add additional components to the spectrum. First, we should keep the frequencies of these additional sinusoids at some distance from the signal frequency; otherwise, masking of the signal frequency will occur and the relative threshold for the sinusoid will increase just as it did with broadband noise. (Note the solitary point in Figure 4-1.) Second, the amplitudes of the other components should not be much different from the component at the signal frequency; otherwise, we again run the risk of masking at the signal frequency caused by an upward or downward spread of masking. For all these reasons, we have explored most carefully a set of equal-amplitude sinusoidal components separated from each other by equal logarithmic frequency intervals, that is, the ratio between successive frequency components is constant. We use logarithmic spacing because we know that, roughly, the critical bandwidths increase linearly with center frequency. Thus, a logarithmic spacing preserves approximately equal spacing along the effective (internal) stimulus dimension. In the following section, we will describe how the number and specific frequency intervals influence the detection of a sinusoid added to the central component of the complex.

NUMBER AND DENSITY OF COMPONENTS IN THE MULTITONAL STANDARD

The simplest experiment designed to probe this question of the best frequency composition for the profile is to vary the number of and frequency spacing between the sinusoidal components of a multitonal complex. We have actually conducted this basic experiment twice, in part, because the results were somewhat surprising (Green, Kidd, & Picardi, 1983; Green, Mason & Kidd, 1984). The results of both experiments can be summarized by the following statements. The detection of a sinusoid, added to the central component of the complex, improves as we increase the number of components in the complex, at least until the frequency ratio between successive components is about 1.1–1.3. If a fixed number of components is used, located symmetrically about the signal frequency on a logarithmic scale, then the more distance between components the better, at least out to the ranges we have explored, namely, 200 to 5000 Hz. These results are surprising because the last summary implies that adding frequency components located at some distance from the signal frequency improves the detection of the sinusoid. Figure 4-2, from Green, Mason, and Kidd, shows the results of this manipulation most clearly. (Figure 4-2 is Figure 2 from Green, Mason, & Kidd, 1984.)

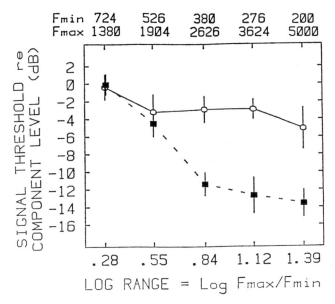

Figure 4-2. Average signal threshold for a signal added to the middle component (1000 Hz) of the complex as a function of the total frequency range of the complex. The data for the three-component complexes are plotted as open circles. The solid points represent data for the conditions in which the number of components varied. The upper abscissa gives the frequency, in Hz, of the lowest and highest frequency of the complex.

The results of two separate experimental manipulations are shown in the figure. Let us consider the results shown by the open points first. In that experiment, the profile is a three-component complex. The center frequency of the complex is 1000 Hz; the two side components are located at equal frequency ratios above and below that frequency. The exact values of the side components are listed across the top of the figure. The signal is an increment in the central component (1000 Hz). The threshold value for this increment relative to the level of the standard 1000-Hz component is the ordinate. The overall level of the sound on each and every presentation is selected from a rectangular distribution (of 1-dB steps), ranging plus and minus 20 dB about a median level of 45 dB. Although the magnitude of the effect is small, it is apparent that increasing the frequency spacing between the three components improves the detectability of an increment in the central component. The data shown in Figure 4-2 are an average over three observers. While the observers varied greatly in absolute sensitivity, all three showed the trends displayed in the figure.

In the second part of the experiment, we varied the number of components in the complex. One complex was a three-component complex with the same narrow frequency spacing used in the first part of the experiment. A second complex was created by adding additional pairs of components to the flanks of this three-component complex. Additional complexes were made by adding to the previous stimulus another pair of flanking components. The total number of components was either 3, 5, 7, 9, or 11. With the 11-component complex, all the frequencies listed above the top of the figure were used. The signal was still an increment in the 1000-Hz component. The same random variation in overall level was used, and the results are plotted using the same measure of signal threshold on the ordinate. Adding an additional 10 components to the standard increases the overall level of the complex by about 10 dB. Despite this increase in overall level, the signal threshold drops by about the same amount. Green, Kidd, and Picardi (1983) found the signal threshold dropped about 13 dB for a similar condition.

Naturally, one is not surprised to find that energy remote from the signal frequency does not make the increment harder to hear. This finding is completely consistent with the way we believe the critical band operates in traditional masking studies. As has been found in many such studies, only energy in a frequency region located near the signal frequency influences the detectability of the signal. What is surprising about our present result is that energy located at a great distance in frequency from the signal *improves* the detectability of the signal. After all, components at 200 and 5000 Hz are many critical bands away from the 1000-Hz component! Yet these remote frequencies are the best ones to employ if only three components constitute the complex. One should also note that the addition of these two components to a set of nine components slightly improves the detectability of the increment in the 1000-Hz signal, as a comparison of the two solid points at the right of the figure shows. Such results as these are completely unlike the results we have seen in more traditional studies of intensity discrimination.

These results are not limited to a single study. Very similar conclusions were drawn from an earlier study by Green, Kidd, and Picardi (1983). There are slight differences in the conditions explored in the two studies. In the earlier study, there was greater range of frequency ratios (density) explored. At a much closer frequency spacing than that explored in Figure 4-2, masking is evident and the threshold value for the signal will increase considerably for any number of components. Also, in the earlier study, the results showed less decrease in signal threshold as component density was increased for the given value of density explored in Figure 4-2. But both studies agree on the effect of the variable density and frequency spacing. In the Green, Kidd, and Picardi study, the best detection occurred with a 21-component complex ranging from 300 to 3000 Hz, a ratio of 1.12 between successive components. As Figure 4-1 shows, the best complex consists of 11 components ranging from 200 to 5000 Hz, a ratio of 1.38 between successive components. Increasing the number of components to 21 components, a ratio of 1.17 between successive components, made the signal threshold increase a few dB. We are uncertain how these differences in the results should best be interpreted. It seems unlikely that the small change in total range is the critical difference. Of course, the observers were different in the two experiments, and it could be that there are differences among observers in the optimum density of component spacing.

The fact that the signal does become harder to hear when the number of components is increased beyond some optimum density means that masking does occur as one moves more and more energy into a frequency region close to the signal. In this respect, the critical band concept works for profile analysis as it does in more traditional intensity discrimination experiments. Increased masking energy in the critical band makes the increment more difficult to detect. The differences arise when we consider energy outside the critical band. In traditional studies, this energy is found to have no effect. The entire thrust of the critical band experiment is that the observer can *ignore* the energy outside the critical band. Thus, only the signal to noise ratio within the critical band influences the detectability of the signal. In profile analysis, a different conclusion seems to emerge. Energy outside the signal frequency region may *improve* the detectability of the increment. This energy must be far enough away to avoid direct masking. The exact frequency distance is uncertain: a width of about 300 Hz at a 1000-Hz center frequency, if we take the optimum number of components to be 11, and a width of about 120 Hz, if we take the optimum number of components to be 21. This would correspond to a spacing of one or two critical bands. All our results suggest that energy located remote from the region near the signal frequency contributes to the definition of the profile.

Initially, we thought there might be an optimum spacing that would contribute to the best simultaneous comparisons. Clearly, one would expect that the best detection would occur only when *independent* frequency regions were compared. Thus, spacings of at least one critical band seemed the most likely candidates. That some local comparison process would be superior to some distant comparisons, such as 200 and 1000 Hz or 1000 and 5000 Hz, seemed self-evident. The results do not support such beliefs. The results suggest that a global comparison process rather than a local comparison process produces the most acute simultaneous determinations. The detection of an increment in the central component is best when the comparison components are as far away in frequency as reasonably possible.

EFFECTS OF LEVEL VARIATION

The preceding sections have established two features of the profile analysis process. First, only the power spectrum of the stimulus is important; phase is of no importance. Second, the simultaneous comparison of two or more parts of the spectrum does not seem to be restricted to neighboring or local regions. Indeed, the results suggest that the comparison process extends over wide-frequency regions and is more accurate when this is the case. Detection of the change in the spectrum, caused by adding the signal to the complex, may involve an evaluation of the shape of the entire spectrum rather than comparing local features. What is impressive about these comparisons of spectral shape is that they are accomplished despite wide variation of the overall level of the sound presentation. On a typical trial, the observer compares two sounds that differ in level by 20 dB or so. How is the comparison mechanism able to compensate for such level variation? Is the quality and accuracy of the comparison process affected in any important way by these variations in level?

To appreciate this issue in more detail, it is necessary to review some of our current ideas about how the spectrum is represented in the auditory system. Almost since the beginning of modern research in psychoacoustics, we have realized that spectral representation and stimulus level are related. In 1924, Wegel and Lane studied what they called masking patterns. Specifically, they measured the audibility of one sinusoid, the signal, in the presence of another sinusoid, the masker. The masker was fixed in level and frequency. The signal was then varied in frequency and adjusted in level until it was just detectable. The resulting curve of these just-audible levels as a function of frequency was called a masking pattern. Two important sets of functional relations were revealed by this early study. First, for maskers near the signal frequency, raising the level of the masker by a certain amount caused a nearly proportional increase in signal level. For maskers that were more remote from the signal frequency, this nearly linear relation was not true. For the remote maskers, the intensity relations were quite complicated and depended on whether the masker was above or below the signal frequency. If the masker was above the frequency of the signal, it produced no masking whatsoever, except at the highest level. If the masker was below the signal frequency, there again was little effect at low levels, but at higher levels the threshold of the signal would be strongly influenced by the level of the masker. At levels where the masker had an effect, raising the level of a low-frequency masker produced enormous increases in the signal threshold. This so-called upward spread of masking was the most obvious and striking feature of the Wegel and Lane masking patterns. It has been confirmed in numerous subsequent studies and is the central theoretical assumption of almost all quantitative treatments of masking.

Later research has treated these masking patterns as the result of a hypothetical concept called an "excitation" pattern. This hypothetical activity is assumed to define certain internal spectra for the listener. The patterns depend on the frequency and intensity of the stimulus and are used to understand and explain the frequency-intensity relations of all signal-masker combinations. The earliest example of such a quantitative treatment is found in the original paper by Wegel and Lane. They used their data to create a set of inferences about how the basilar membrane must respond to different combinations of frequency and intensity. The more recent use of this concept has been that of Whitfield (1967) and Zwicker (1958, 1970). Zwicker has developed an elaborate theoretical structure based on this concept and has employed these ideas in explaining a wide variety of psychoacoustic phenomena. A computational procedure for calculating the loudness of a complex spectra has been proposed by Zwicker, and this procedure has been adopted as an international standard for the prediction of the loudness of impulsive noise (ISO Rec. 532).

A recent revision of this theory has been presented by Florentine and Buus (1981). They have proposed that decisions about the changes in the shape of these excitation patterns are accomplished by a statistically optimum combination rule. Change in any part of the spectrum is integrated with changes in other parts to arrive at a final decision. They then apply this modification to a variety of masking tasks and demonstrate the superiority of this model to the earlier versions that assumed a change in the spectrum was detected on the basis of change in a single channel. All these theories stress the nonlinear relation between the shape of the excitation patterns and the level of the stimulus. Recall our earlier discussion of the near-miss to Weber's law. One account was based on the nonlinear growth of the excitation level at the higher frequency regions with increases in stimulus level. Thus, the increment in the sinusoid becomes more and more detectable, because a fixed increment produces a greater change in excitation patterns at the higher levels, as well as a greater spread of excitation over frequency, thus broadening the excitation patterns.

In effect, these ideas mean that the shape of the internal spectrum is level dependent. The form of the excitation pattern does not simply scale with the level of the stimulus; rather, it changes shape as the stimulus level changes. Consequently, a very natural question is whether or not these changes in internal shape affect the observer's ability to detect a change in the shape of the external spectrum.

While the question may be an easy one to ask, it is difficult to predict what the answer will be. To appreciate this uncertainty, we must realize that this issue is related to the more general topic of perceptual constancy and is, like many areas of perception, one of some subtlety. Let us consider this question with an analogy from the field of visual perception. Suppose we were studying judgments about the heights of objects, for example, the heights of people. In conducting these experiments, we might make all the judgments at a constant viewing distance. In that case, the visual angle subtended by different people would be nearly the same on the observer's retina. Alternatively, we might have the observer make the judgments about the people's heights when they are viewed at different distances. In the latter case, since the visual angle depends on viewing distance, a taller person seen at a greater distance may well produce a smaller visual angle than a shorter person seen at a nearer distance. The internal (retinal) representation of height must then vary with viewing distance in the same way that our internal spectrum depends on stimulus level. Suppose the accuracy of the judgments about height were largely independent of differences in viewing distance. We call this ability to judge size independent of viewing distance size constancy. Indeed, there are a variety of so-called perceptual constancies. All involve the principle that one can accurately assess some aspect of the external stimulus, despite systematic alterations of the internal representation. The remarkable thing about the constancies is that this ability to ignore the irrelevant internal variability is automatic and unconscious. Despite its unconscious nature, the resulting percept often reflects the external attribute with considerable accuracy. In fact, careful analytic study of the sensory system is required to realize that some kind of compensation for the irrelevant aspect is needed, that is, there is a perceptual constancy at work.

Thus, no matter what effect level variation has on the ability to detect a change in a complex spectrum, we are ready with an answer. If, on the one hand, level variation has some effect, then we will not be surprised because we know that systematic alterations of the internal spectra occur with changes in stimulus level. If, on the other hand, the level variation has little effect, then we will claim that a perceptual constancy exists. The auditory system can compensate for the systematic alteration of the internal spectral representation and make accurate judgments about the external spectrum. What is somewhat novel about this constancy, if it exists, is that the system must compensate for a highly nonlinear change. Often, in visual constancies, one simply needs to linearly re-scale the basic sensory data to achieve an accurate representation of the external stimulus. Our Dutch colleagues have suggested that profile analysis is simply the ability to discriminate changes in the timbre of a sound. Thus, if the results appear to support a constancy principle, we could call it "timbre constancy." Let us now leave the world of speculation and perceptual terminology and see how changes in overall level actually affect the ability to detect alterations in the power spectra.

EXPERIMENTS ON LEVEL VARIATION

The general level of interest in this topic is indicated by the number of people who participated in the published investigation (Mason, Kidd, Hanna, & Green, 1984). The first part of their study established that the absolute level of the sound presentation had a relatively small effect on the observer's ability to detect a change in the spectra. Five median levels of sound presentation were investigated: 30, 40, 50, 60, and 70 dB SPL. At each of these levels, a 10-dB range of level variation was imposed and the detectability of an increase in level of the central component of a 21-

component complex was measured. The only change in the ability to detect the increment was a slight superiority for the middle levels, 50 and 60 dB. There was little change in the threshold for the increment over the five conditions. The greatest threshold difference, measured in terms of signal level re the component level of the profile, was about 3 dB. Nor were any changes in performance even monotonic with presentation level. This latter result is important, because it establishes that the quality of the detection process does not improve as we change overall presentation level. The near-miss to Weber's law does not seem to hold for profile analysis, unlike the results obtained when detecting an increment in a single sinusoidal signal. In the next chapter, we will address these differences more directly. For the present, we can assume that the accuracy of the profile analysis process is roughly independent of the stimulus level, perhaps being slightly better in the middle of the 30- to 70-dB range.

Next, Mason et al. fixed the median level at 50 dB per component and randomly varied the overall level over a 60-dB range. Each presentation level was chosen at random from this rectangular distribution of intensities, 20 to 80 dB, in 1-dB steps. On each trial, the presentation level in each interval was recorded along with the listener's response. Four observers listened to nearly 5000 trials so that a detailed, post-hoc analysis of this data could be performed. The major item of interest was whether or not the difference in presentation level heard on a given trial influenced the probability of a correct judgment. To address this issue, the trials were categorized on the basis of the difference in sound level heard in the two intervals of the forced-choice trial. For each level difference, which obviously includes trials occurring at many different absolute levels, we tabulated the percentage of correct judgments. The data are shown in Figure 4-3. The data indicate that level differences as large or small as 40 dB had remarkably little effect on the accuracy of the judgments. Only extreme level differences of 50 or 60 dB appear to worsen detection performance to a statistically significant degree.

It should also be noted that the dependent variable in this experiment is an extremely sensitive measure of detection accuracy. Roughly speaking, we find that a 5% change in detection occurs for a 1-dB change in signal level. Thus, the central portion of the graph shows performance changes less than plus and minus 1 dB, despite 40-dB changes in the level of the spectra to be compared. This is an impressive demonstration of a perceptual constancy. Furthermore, the drop in percent correct of 20 to 25% reflects, at most, a decrease of 4 to 5 dB. Part of this decrease can be attributed to a "loudness bias." A decomposition of the data into a set of linear weights revealed a response bias to select the louder interval as containing the signal. This bias will lead to poor performance if the non-signal sound is presented at a high level, and such a circumstance can only occur when the level difference is extreme. Thus, the performance level at these extreme stimulus levels may be slightly inferior to that

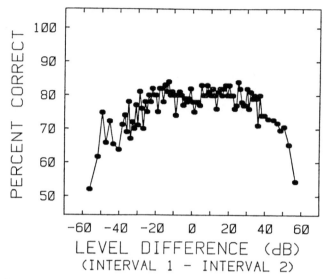

Figure 4-3. Post-hoc analysis of the percentage of correct responses in a two-alternative forced-choice task as a function of the level difference in the stimuli presented in the two intervals on a single trial. Average data over four observers and about 18,000 observations are presented. The flat portion of the function represents the range of "level constancy."

observed at the middle stimulus levels. Support for this theory is provided from a small informal experiment in which the range of stimulus difference was 60 rather than 40 dB. The results showed the decrease in performance only over the last 5 to 10 dB of stimulus difference. The data were essentially flat for the plus or minus 40-dB differences. But, even if the decrease in performance is attributable only to difference in stimulus level, the constancy effect extends over differences of at least 40 dB in stimulus level.

In summary, we have learned several properties about the profile analysis mechanism. First, it is phase insensitive. The basic stimulus for the profile comparison process is the power spectrum of the stimulus. Next, the comparison process does not appear restricted to some narrow frequency range such as one or two critical bands. Rather, the best comparisons appear to occur with wide-frequency spacing—five or ten critical bands appear better than one or two. Increasing the number of components increases the accuracy of the comparison process as long as masking of the signal component is avoided. Finally, the comparison process appears to be able to assess the shape of the external spectrum, despite sizable changes in overall level. A kind of spectral shape constancy exists over at least a 40-dB range.

5

Frequency and Relative Level Effects in Profile Analysis

In previous chapters, we learned how detecting a change in the shape of a complex spectrum must depend on estimating and comparing intensity level at different frequency regions of the spectra. Neither the phase nor the absolute level of the waveform appears to influence the ability to detect such change to any great degree. The frequency spacing and density of the components in the spectra, however, do appear to influence the ability to detect an increment in a single component. In this chapter, we will explore two additional questions. First, does the frequency region where the change takes place strongly influence the ability to detect the change? Alternatively, are changes in an essentially flat spectrum easiest to detect at high, medium, or low frequency regions? Second, does the relative level of the altered component re the background components strongly influence the ability to detect a change? Alternatively, must the levels of the compared components be at essentially the same intensity level, or can the comparison process detect changes even if the initial intensity levels are quite different? Finally, we end this chapter with a report of some measurements on the ability to detect a change in the intensity of a single sinusoid in two conditions. In the first condition, no other components are present in the spectrum (classical Weber experiment). In the second condition, many other components are present (optimum profile conditions). For observers previously trained in profile conditions, the given change is more detectable when other components are present in the spectrum. We take up the question of the frequency region of the change first.

EFFECTS OF SIGNAL FREQUENCY REGION

The experimental question is very simple. Suppose we have a set of components that have equal amplitudes and are equally spaced on a logarithmic frequency axis over an appreciable frequency range. The signal to be detected is an increase in the intensity of a single component. Does the frequency of this signal component make any difference to the observer's ability to detect the change? As with all these experiments, the overall level of the sounds is varied on each presentation so that the signal must be detected as a relative change in the spectral background, not simply as a measure of absolute intensity at the single, signal frequency. Clearly, such a task necessitates an estimate and comparison of *at least* two intensity levels, one at the signal component and the other at one or more of the nonsignal components. How are such intensity estimates made? Do these estimates depend on the frequency of the component being considered? These are some of the questions that we will consider in this section.

The background to these experiments has a very long history in auditory theory. The classical theories of how pitch is coded—namely, the place and temporal theories of hearing—also commented on how acoustic intensity is estimated. Both theories suggested that intensity was coded on the basis of the amount and vigor of the neural activity. If such were the case, then it should matter little to either theory whether the signal component that is being altered in intensity is a high- or low-frequency component. Recent consideration of how the auditory system codes a complex waveform such as that produced in speech has raised new issues in this area. To understand these problems in more detail requires a brief review of the neural responses observed at the peripheral level of the auditory system and some speculation about how intensity is coded for complex acoustic spectra such as typical vowel waveforms.

PERIPHERAL NEURAL CODING

As we reviewed in an earlier chapter, the presence of a sinusoid stimulates a range of fibers located at a particular point along the basilar membrane. The lateral extent of the activity grows with increasing intensity, so that a weak sinusoid activates a restricted region and a strong sinusoid activates a much greater extent along the basilar membrane. Thus, a more intense sinusoid activates a much wider range of fibers, each of which is specially sensitive to a given frequency of stimulation. A more intense sinusoid also activates a greater number of fibers at any single place, because of the slight staggering in threshold levels discussed earlier. Both of these mechanisms may be responsible for the perception of a louder sinusoid. Both mechanisms are essentially consistent with the modern view of the place theory of hearing. According to this view, the rate and number of fibers active when a given sound is present code the intensity of the sound. We call this the "discharge rate" theory of intensity coding, following Sachs and Young (1979), because it emphasizes that firing rate is the primary parameter of the neural activity to mirror changes in intensity. But what of the temporal properties of the neural discharge?

At lower frequencies, the fiber is known to be sensitive to the phase of the stimulus in the sense that the fiber is more or less likely to produce a neural discharge, an impulse or spike, at a certain phase of the stimulating waveform. There are different procedures used to demonstrate the presence of phase locking. One technique is to stimulate with a periodic signal and record when a neural impulse occurs with respect to the time within the period of the waveform. The collection of such times is then used to construct what is known as a "period histogram." At low frequencies, such period histograms show that a fiber is more likely to fire during a particular period of the stimulating waveform and less likely to fire at other times. Such asymmetry is evidence of phase locking.

Although the period histogram is a very useful tool for neurophysiological analysis, we will emphasize a slightly different method of analysis. In this technique, called a "post-stimulus histogram," one simply records the time interval between successive nerve impulses. The data produced by such analyses are somewhat easier to interpret in terms of a neural mechanism or model of intensity coding, because the basic information, namely, the time between successive impulses, is a quantity clearly present in the nervous system and one it may be able to use. Interpreting a period histogram in terms of a neural mechanism is somewhat more difficult, because the histogram requires knowledge of the phase of the stimulus in its construction. The difference between the two methods of analysis should not be overemphasized, however, because the information contained in either a period or interval histogram is very closely related.

For lower frequency tones, the poststimulus interval histogram distributions tend to have a definite multimodal character, with the modes being centered on the period of the stimulating sinusoid. Figure 5-1, taken from the Wisconsin group, illustrates a series of such distributions recorded from the same auditory fiber when driven by a 1111-Hz sinusoid at several different intensities. The small dots located under the modes of the distribution are the times of successive periods of the waveform. The intense stimuli, presented at the top of the graph, show clear phase locking. As the intensity diminishes, the peaks of the distribution diminish in amplitude and the degree of phase locking also diminishes. The decrease in amplitude reflects the fact that the discharge rate of the fiber decreases as the intensity of the stimulation is diminished. The decrease in the peakedness of the multimodal distribution reflects the diminution in phase locking.

A simple way to try to quantify these observations about the peakedness of these distributions is to first create a "normalized" histogram by dividing the number of spikes observed at any time interval by the total number of discharges used to create the histogram. The abscissa of such

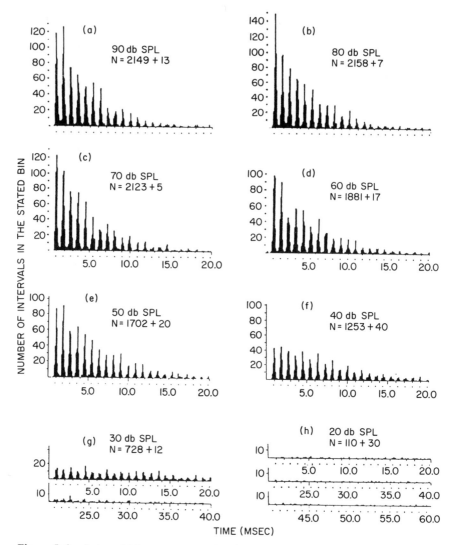

139
140
141
142
143
144
145
146
147
172

Figure 5-1. Interval histogram recorded from a single auditory nerve fiber. The different panels of the graph represent different intensities for the sinusoidal signal, whose frequency is 1111 Hz (= 900 μsec). Each entry in the histogram represents a time between successive neural impulses. The value of N is the sum of two numbers. The first is the total number of intervals recorded in the time indicated along the abscissa; the second number is the number of intervals that exceeded that value. Note that at the lower intensity levels the time scale has been extended. The peaks of the multimodal distribution occur at the period of the sinusoid. (From Rose et al., 1967.)

a normalized histogram would then range between zero and unity, and the sum of abscissa values integrated over all time intervals would equal one. The degree of phase locking in such a normalized distribution could be estimated by simply computing a Fourier transform of this histogram. The relative magnitudes of the frequencies in this transform would provide an estimate of the degree of phase locking. For example, the transform of the histogram in the upper left corner of Figure 1-1 will clearly have a very large magnitude at the frequency of the signal, since there is strong periodicity in the histogram at the reciprocal of that frequency. The magnitude at other frequencies will be much smaller. If there is little periodicity apparent, as in the histograms in the lower right of the figure, than all the components of the Fourier series will be roughly equal in size. The relative magnitude of the transform at the signal frequency, compared to the magnitudes of the other components, will then provide an index of the degree of phase locking.

Young and Sachs (1979), using the period histogram, have carried out an extensive series of studies of how the peripheral auditory fibers respond when stimulated by a periodic vowel stimulus. Their primary interest was to determine how the peripheral nervous system represents a complex auditory stimulus such as that present in the speech wave. As we know (see the discussion of tuning curves in Chapter 2), each fiber is tuned to a particular frequency region. It is, therefore, possible to construct a kind of "neural spectrogram" by simply sampling from a number of different fibers. The frequency axis of this spectrogram would be the characteristic or best frequency of the fiber. The ordinate of the spectrogram should represent some measure of the fibers' neural activity that reflects the intensity of the stimulus. At least two neural measures naturally recommend themselves. The first measure is simply *firing rate,* and it was used in their first study where they constructed what we will call "firing rate spectrograms" for several vowel stimuli. The major finding of that study (Sachs & Young, 1979) was that these firing rate spectrograms tended to lose detail as the intensity of the vowel stimulus was increased. At low intensity level, these firing rate spectrograms showed clear peaks and valleys proving a reasonable representation of the major formants of the vowel. At higher intensity levels, these peaks and valleys disappeared and the formants were no longer evident. Thus, they rejected firing rate as the major representation of stimulus intensity.

Next, they computed a synchronization index for each fiber, obtained from the Fourier series approximation to the period histograms (Young & Sachs, 1979). This measure, similar to the one discussed above, provides a quantity that is related to the phase locking of the fiber to those stimulus components within the frequency region to which that fiber is tuned. Again, by sampling a larger number of fibers, it is possible to construct a picture of what we might call a "synchronization spectrogram." The coordinates of this spectrogram are the best frequency of the fiber as the abscissa and the synchronization measure as the ordinate to represent the intensity of the stimulus. Over a stimulus range of 50 dB, these synchronization spectrograms provide a nearly invariant representation of the vowel stimulus. The formant peaks are evident, both at the lowest intensity level, approximately 35 dB, and at the highest levels, approximately 85 dB. The similarity of these spectrograms over a wide range of stimulus levels is indeed impressive. Thus, Sachs and Young conclude that the degree of phase locking may be a more important and useful measure of stimulus intensity, especially for complex stimuli, than simple firing rate. Let us now take these ideas and consider them with respect to our profile analysis task.

PROFILES WITH SIGNALS
AT DIFFERENT FREQUENCIES

The simplest experiment to perform is to start with a flat spectra, a set of components all equal in amplitude. The signal is produced by making an increment in a single component, a single bump in this otherwise flat spectrum. Is the detection of such a change strongly dependent on the frequency at which the bump occurs? If firing rate is the primary and important code for stimulus intensity, then the frequency location of the signal should matter little, because we know from other data that firing rates vary in much the same way with stimulus intensity at all frequencies. If temporal synchronization is the primary cue, however, the ability to detect the bump should vanish at the higher frequencies, because phase locking—and, hence, any temporal code—is lost at those high frequencies.

While the basic motivation behind the experiment is simple, there are many technical problems that cloud the interpretation of such an experiment. First, we have the question of what is the upper frequency limit of phase locking. At what frequencies should we expect one to lose the ability to detect intensity changes in a high frequency spectra? Like many abilities, phase locking does not fail abruptly at some specific frequency; instead, the degree of phase locking diminishes gradually with frequency. Indeed, the exact upper limit is hard to establish experimentally because the exact characteristics of the recording equipment play an important role in determining this frequency value (Anderson, 1973). Also, the upper limit of phase locking appears to depend somewhat on the species of animal studied, and, hence, firm estimates in humans are lacking. Second, a host of practical problems are associated with the use of high-frequency stimuli. The response of the headphone diminishes at the higher frequencies, and the audibility of such stimuli decreases. All the myriad factors make the interpretation of the results obtained with signals of different frequency difficult. What could be a critical test of the physiological notions becomes an ambiguous result whose final interpretation lies mainly in the eyes of the beholder. But let us describe the data we have.

The first study of this issue is reported in the paper of Green and Mason (1985). They used a 21-component complex, with equal amplitude for each component and the frequencies equally spaced in logarithmic frequency between 200 and 5000 Hz. The signal was an increment in a single component. The median level of a component in the complex was 60 dB SPL. The exact intensity level on any presentation was chosen from a rectangular distribution with a range of 20 dB. The data from the three observers are highly variable and they differ from one another as a function of frequency. One observer's data show elevated thresholds above about 2000 Hz; another observer has good high frequency thresholds with very poor thresholds for the low frequency signals. The average of the three observers' thresholds shows a gentle bowl-shape function, when plotted as a function of signal frequency with the minimum of the bowl at about 1000 Hz and the two sides elevated about 7 to 10 dB with respect to this minimum. The authors report that these observers had previous listening experience at 1000 Hz. Although considerable practice was given at all the frequencies tested, it is conceivable that the minimum was the result of extensive past experience listening to that frequency region.

The first study we undertook when the laboratory was moved to Florida was to measure this same function on a group of naive listeners. These observers had no prior listening experience of any kind in the laboratory setting. The conditions were similar to those used by Green and Mason—21 components ranging from 200 to 5000 Hz. The amplitudes of all components were equal, at 50 dB SPL. The frequency ratio between successive components was the same (equal logarithmic frequency spacing). The overall level of the sound was randomly varied according to a rectangular distribution with a range of 20 dB. Six observers were tested and the average thresholds as a function of signal frequency are shown in Figure 5-2. Each observer's threshold was estimated from 12 adaptive-threshold runs of 50 trials each. The standard error of the mean was calculated on the basis of 72 determinations at each frequency, with six observers and twelve thresholds for each observer. All observers show much the same function, and the mean data are probably our best summary of the results as a function of signal frequency. Again, the data can be described as a bowl-shaped function with the minimum in the 1000- to 2000-Hz region. The elevation in threshold at the high and low frequencies is about 7 to 8 dB.

The data certainly do not provide strong support for a temporal theory of intensity coding. To account for this data, one first must claim that a signal frequency of 4256 Hz is simply not high enough to show the effects of the decline in temporal synchrony. Such a claim may be true, but it certainly represents a rather generous assumption about the upper limit

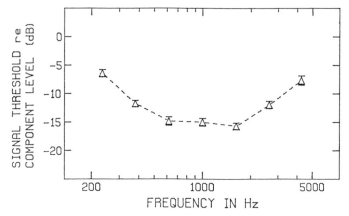

Figure 5-2. The threshold for detecting a single increment in multicomponent complex. The ordinate gives the signal threshold in terms of the signal-to-standard ratio in decibels. The complex extends from 200 to 5000 Hz and consists of 21 equal-amplitude components. The frequency of the signal, an increment in a single component, is indicated along the abscissa.

of phase locking. Further, even if this somewhat dubious claim is correct, it cannot account for the higher thresholds at the lower frequencies, so some additional factors must be introduced to account for the data in that frequency range. A simpler summary is to hold that the function is essentially flat, with the elevated thresholds caused by the extreme ranges of frequencies. The upper frequency rise is caused by the phones, and the lower frequency rise is caused by the poorer audibility of those frequencies in a typical listening environment. The latter is somewhat weak, since the tests were conducted in double-walled acoustic chambers.

It is also possible that the position of the signal within the set of components in the complex is critical. Perhaps the middle component of a complex is simply the position within the spectra where the smallest change can be detected. Detecting a bump at either end of the complex is more difficult, because the comparison process is unidirectional and this is, for some reason, not as precise as a bidirectional comparison. In an attempt to avoid completely this issue of position within the complex, and to achieve more experimental leverage on this problem, we conducted the following experiment.

The complex was a set of only five components with a ratio between the frequencies of successive components of 1.14. The standard or background complex has all five components at the same amplitude. The signal is another complex of five components that produces a ripple in the amplitude spectra of the standard, that is, the first, third, and fifth components are increased in level, whereas the second and fourth are decreased in level. This type of signal was chosen because it is easier to detect than a change in a single component. Detection performance with

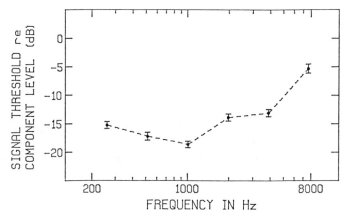

Figure 5-3. Similar to Figure 5-2 except the multicomponent complex consists of 300 components extending from 200 to 10,000 Hz. The signal is a change in five adjacent components of the complex; the odd compnents are increased and the even components decreased. The frequency of the middle component of five is plotted along the abscissa. The ordinate is the signal-to-standard ratio for a single component.

a change in a single component with only five components in the standard is not very good, as we know from our study of component density. The detection of this ripple was then measured as we vary the frequency location of the five components. At the lowest frequency condition, the middle component of the five was 345 Hz, and at the highest frequency, the middle component of the complex was 7567 Hz. Figure 5-3 shows the threshold for the ripple as a function of the frequency of the middle component of the five-component complex. Although the data do show a larger elevation in threshold at the higher frequencies, the amount is still surprisingly small if temporal synchrony in the peripheral fiber is the basis for estimating the intensity level of the components. At the highest frequency, almost everyone would agree that temporal synchrony is nearly impossible. Thus, it should be virtually impossible to detect a ripple in a complex spectra at any level. Once more, the simpler summary would seem to describe the results of frequency as essentially flat with elevation at the extreme frequencies due to other causes related to the audibility of these extreme frequency components.

PROFILE AND SIGNAL INTENSITY DIFFERENCES: PEDESTAL EFFECTS

In many of the profile experiments, we use a multicomponent complex as the standard spectra with all components equal in intensity. The signal is often an increase in the intensity of a single component of the standard spectra. Because of the random variation in overall intensity level on each presentation, detecting such a change must involve a simultaneous comparison of the *standard* intensity level with the *signal* intensity level, that is, a comparison of the intensity level at a nonsignal component(s) with the intensity level at the signal component. In effect, the detection task reduces to the question of whether this difference in intensity level is zero or slightly greater than zero. The experimental question we now wish to address is whether or not the quality of the detection performance depends on this initial intensity difference being near zero. Suppose the level of the signal component were 10 dB greater than the level at the standard. Would the detection of a small increment in this level difference, the signal, be impaired by this initial difference of 10 dB? If we think of the stimulus in the frequency domain, then we can envision any initial difference in intensity level between the signal component and the other components of the spectra, the standard, as a pedestal at the signal component. The signal is then added to this pedestal. The experimental question is how does the level of this pedestal re the components of the standard affect the threshold of the signal?

We need not restrict our investigation to pedestals that increase the level at the signal component. We may also decrease the relative level of the pedestal compared to the level of the standard components to determine if the detection of the signal is impaired by this manipulation as well. Clearly, at extreme pedestal-to-standard ratios, these experimental manipulations are bound to have some effect. If the pedestal is very large, compared with the standard, then the standard will be virtually inaudible and any comparison between pedestal and standard amplitude will be impaired. Similarly, if the pedestal is very small with respect to the standard, then the larger standard components will mask the signal frequency and the detection of the signal will be impaired. The real issue, then, is over what range of pedestal amplitudes does detection of the signal remain relatively unchanged? In effect, we are studying the tolerance in the comparison process for an initial intensity difference.

We must confess at the outset that we know less than we should about this important experimental variable. One of the problems is that introducing any change from an equal-amplitude standard usually leads initially to poorer detection performance. The thresholds will generally improve once the novelty of the situation has worn off, but it is difficult to know when the effects of practice are at asymptotic levels. Thus, threshold values are difficult to estimate with confidence. Green and Kidd (1983) have published the only empirical investigation on this topic. Their results suggest that the comparison process is reasonably tolerant. The specific values appear to depend on the frequency spacing among the components of the spectra. We warn the reader that these results have not been replicated, and we present them here as our only available evidence.

Green and Kidd used different numbers of components for the equal-amplitude standard. The median level of the components of the standard was 45 dB SPL and the level presented on any single presentation varied according to a rectangular distribution over a range of 40 dB. The frequency of the signal component, about 950 Hz, was always in the middle of the standard complex on a logarithmic frequency scale. The number of components in the standard complex ranged from 2 to 20. In the middle of this complex spectra was a pedestal to which the signal would be added. In different experimental conditions, the pedestal amplitude was varied in 6 dB steps from -18 to $+24$ dB re the standard components. We express the signal threshold level re the *pedestal* level, since Weber's law is almost exactly true for profile conditions, as we will see in a later section.

We know from our previous study that the detection of the signal will be much better when the standard spectra has more components. This difference can amount to 10 to 12 dB when we change from 3 to 21 components. In an attempt to make the detectability of the signals more nearly similar, Green and Kidd varied the frequency ratio between successive components of the spectrum as the total number of components in the spectrum was altered. The logarithm of the ratio between successive components was equal to the reciprocal of $(N + 1)$, where N is the number of components in the standard, excluding the pedestal. Thus, for example, if the number of standard components was 20, the logarithm of the ratio is 0.0476, and the ratio between successive frequencies is 1.1158. This places the lowest and highest components at 200 and 3000 Hz. If only two standard components are used, the lowest component is about 440 Hz and the highest about 2000 Hz, with the pedestal at the signal frequency of about 950 Hz. Confounding stimulus number and density in this way did make the signal threshold more nearly equal in the different conditions. But this manipulation is only partially successful, and this fact should be appreciated when attempting to assess the effects of changes in pedestal level over the different conditions.

Figure 5-4 shows the experimental results. The ordinate is the pedestal to standard ratio, the level of the initial level at the signal component re the level of the other components of the standard. The abscissa is the signal level at threshold re the pedestal level. With 20 components in the standard spectra, the signal threshold is best when the pedestal is 6 dB greater than the standard. The threshold rises as we decrease the level of the pedestal from that value. If we increase the pedestal level, the signal again becomes more difficult to detect but only by a slight amount. The same general pattern is evident for the 10-compound standard. The range of the better detection performance appears to be somewhat larger. For the lesser number of components, the general U-shaped function becomes even broader and only the extreme pedestal-to-standard ratios suggest any deterioration whatsoever in signal threshold.

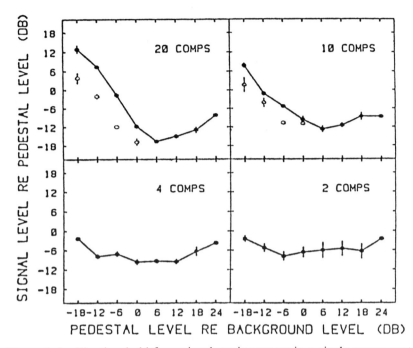

Figure 5-4. The threshold for a signal, an increment in a single component of the complex, as a function of the pedestal level. The pedestal level (the component to which the signal is added) is expressed re the level of the other components of the complex along the abscissa. The threshold is expressed as the signal-to-pedestal ratio in decibels along the ordinate. The data are presented for different numbers of components in the multicomponent complex (solid symbols). The signal, or pedestal, frequency was always the central component of the complex, approximately 950 Hz. The open circles represent data obtained when we remove the component of the standard immediately below the signal frequency. The improvement in threshold (solid circles minus open circles) indicates that at least part of the increase in masking at the weaker pedestal levels occurs because of simple masking. (From Green & Kidd, 1983.)

Presumably, the left side of the U-shaped function occurs, in part, because of simple masking. This explanation provides a reason for why the complexes with more components show a greater increase in signal threshold when we decrease the pedestal level. The standards with more components have more components nearer the signal frequency and hence are more effective maskers. The frequency spacing between components is greater for the standards with the lesser number of components; thus, the amount of masking is minimized. If we remove the two frequencies just below the signal frequency from the 20-component standard, then the points marked by open circles are obtained for the pedestal levels less than or equal to the standard level. Similar data are presented for the 10-component standard when a single component—the one just below the frequency of the signal—is removed. Clearly, these results suggest that masking is at least a partial explanation of the asymmetry in the U-shaped function that describes the results. If masking could be completely removed, the results might well be summarized by stating that the effect of pedestal level is unimportant as long as it is within ± 12 dB of the standard level. On the basis of this data, we would conclude that the comparison process involved in profile analysis is tolerant of at least 12-dB differences in initial level. Once this difference is exceeded, the signal becomes more difficult to hear. The amount of elevation in threshold is relatively slight if the pedestal is increased in level over the standard. More elevation in signal threshold is evident when the pedestal is reduced in level, in large part because of the effects of masking.

PROFILE ANALYSIS VERSUS
SIMPLE INTENSITY DISCRIMINATION

In the concluding section of this chapter, we take up the issue of the relative acuity of discriminating a change in the shape of a complex spectrum versus the acuity of detecting a change in absolute intensity level. In the preceding chapters, we have tried to make the case that two separate and distinct processes may be involved in hearing a change in the intensity spectrum of an auditory signal. The first we call pure intensity discrimination; this process detects a change in absolute intensity level. The acuity of this process can be measured in tasks where the spectrum of the signal does not change its shape but is simply altered in level. In such a situation, the basic comparison process must be one of *successive* comparisons of two intensity levels measured at two different times. We have contrasted this process with the detection of a change in the shape of the complex auditory spectrum, what we have called profile analysis. In detecting a change in spectral shape, the comparison process must be one of *simultaneous* comparisons of intensity levels at different regions of the spectrum because random variation in level over time renders the absolute level an ineffective cue. What system can hear the smallest intensity change, the simultaneous or the successive comparison process? We hasten to point out that our interest in this question is not simply theoretical. In many realistic situations, because the absolute level of the sound is relatively constant, both cues are available. Thus, both simultaneous and successive comparisons could be used and both are effective detection strategies. Presumably, in these situations, the observer uses the more sensitive system. To predict performance in a variety of realistic situations, one would have to know the relative sensitivity of the two systems.

Little data are available on this issue, in part because detection of a change in spectral shape has only recently been the subject of experimental study. Comparison of detection performance in the two situations is also complicated by the issue of prior training and experience. Our impression is that there is remarkably little transfer of training between the two detection skills. Observers with a long history of training in pure intensity-discrimination experiments often do very poorly when first confronted by a task involving the detection of a change in spectral shape. Similarly, observers well practiced in detecting changes in spectral shape often find detection of simple intensity changes initially difficult. Recently, I heard a well-trained profile observer complain, when asked to discriminate a change in the intensity of a single sinusoid, that the only thing you could listen for was a change in loudness!

A second factor that makes comparison of the detection performance in the two tasks difficult is that there is considerable range in the ability of different people to hear simple changes in intensity level. The variability in the Weber fraction for intensity changes of pure tones was discussed in Chapter 3. While there is an impression of great similarity between the performance levels of different individuals, this impression is created largely by the use of very compressive measures of the Weber fraction. One often hears, for example, that the level difference is about 1 dB. What is not appreciated is that a change from 0.5 to 1.5 dB corresponds to a 12 dB change on the scale of signal-to-background level that we have commonly used in this monograph. Our review of the previous studies of the pure-tone Weber fractions indicated considerable variability in the absolute levels of performance, probably caused by large differences in the acuity of the individual observers. It is likely that there is a similar range of differences in the ability of individuals to detect changes in a spectral profile. Such differences have not been extensively studied.

A final complication is that the observers used in most of the profile tasks are not a random selection from the population, but are screened in various ways. Some observers find it extremely difficult to hear the change in shape of a complex spectrum. While they improve with practice, it does not appear likely that they will ever be useful participants in a series of experiments involving the comparison of thresholds obtained in a variety of experimental conditions. Our usual procedure is to train and test subjects over a period of one or two days on the detection of an increment in a 1000-Hz tone in an 11- or 21-component complex. If performance does not reach the -10- to -20-dB-range at the end of three days, then we dismiss the subject. In general, we believe that practically all subjects could be trained to reach this level of performance, but if more than three days are required we feel that such observers would need an excessive amount of training throughout the various conditions of the experiment. Since other subjects can be found that require less training, these are the observers we prefer. We also have a bias to select subjects with some musical training. Little hard data exist on the benefit of such past experience, but some of our best observers have played musical instruments, particularly string instruments such as the violin or guitar which require careful tuning.

One direct comparison of the relative ability of two groups of subjects on both tasks has been published (Green & Mason, 1985). They compared two groups of observers—five experienced in profile listening, five who were not. The five inexperienced profile listeners had considerable training in tasks that could be classified as pure intensity-discrimination tasks. The thresholds for the ten observers were measured in two detection tasks: a pure intensity-discrimination task and a profile task.

The pure intensity-discrimination task was the detection of a change in the level of a 1000-Hz sinusoid. The sinusoid was presented at a level of 40 dB SPL. The profile task was the detection of the change in the intensity of that same component, but the 1000-Hz component was surrounded by 10 other components. We used the familiar, 11-component complex (200–5000 Hz). All components were equal in intensity and presented at the 40 dB SPL level. Unlike the bulk of the experiments we have reported, there was no variation in overall intensity of the sounds from trial to trial. The component level of the complex was 40 dB on each and every presentation. The ratio of the frequencies between successive components of the complex was approximately 1.38. Thus, the two neighbors to the 1000-Hz component had frequencies of 1379 and 724 Hz. The signal duration in both tasks was 100 msec. The thresholds were estimated from the mean of 6 runs of 50 adaptive trials (2 down-1 up). Table 5-1 presents the thresholds estimated in the two tasks for the ten observers.

As can be seen in the table, the best detection performance averages about −17 dB, but it occurs for different conditions for the two groups.

Table 5-1. Entry is the relative signal threshold in dB (standard error of estimate)

Observers	Single Sinusoid	Profile	Diff (SS-P)
Profile experienced			
1	−10.5 (1.4)	−18.6 (1.7)	8.1
2	−6.4 (2.0)	−13.6 (0.6)	7.2
3	−12.0 (0.8)	−18.5 (1.3)	6.5
4	−11.2 (1.3)	−15.8 (1.2)	4.6
5	−18.0 (1.5)	−22.7 (2.3)	4.7
Mean	−11.6 (1.4)	−17.8 (1.4)	6.2
Profile inexperienced			
6	−20.0 (1.6)	−10.9 (2.2)	−9.1
7	−13.2 (2.0)	−12.3 (1.6)	−0.9
8	−19.7 (1.0)	−9.2 (1.3)	−10.5
9	−14.0 (1.0)	−10.0 (1.6)	−4.0
10	−17.4 (0.8)	−20.2 (1.4)	+2.8
Mean	−16.9 (1.6)	−12.5 (1.6)	−4.3

For the experienced profile listeners, it occurs in the profile conditions. For the inexperienced profile listeners, it occurs in the single sinusoid condition. The average difference between performance on the favored and unfavored task is also very similar in the two groups—about 5 dB. The pattern of interaction between past listening experience and the two detection tasks, evident in the average thresholds, is reflected to a greater or lesser degree by every individual observer with the exception of Observer 9. That observer, whose performance level is good on both tasks, is somewhat better on the profile task, despite the lack of previous experience.

According to the summary made by Rabinowitz et al. (1976), the average threshold for the single sinusoid condition should be about −19 dB. This is about 2 dB lower than the average threshold obtained by the inexperienced profile listeners. Presumably, with enough training, the profile listeners could achieve similar levels, but we have no data on that issue as yet. Informally, we tried to improve the performance of the inexperienced profile listeners in the profile task. But their thresholds, after an additional 2000 trials, did not improve very much. We are still uncertain about this result. The interaction present in the data reflects either a difference in training or a difference in the observers. It may be that differences in past experience can simply not be overcome by a few thousand trials. Alternatively, there may simply be two different types of observers. One group, relatively poor at pure intensity discrimination tasks, benefits from the possibility of making simultaneous comparisons between different components. Another group, relatively poor at making simultaneous comparisons, is acute at making successive loudness judgments.

The effects of training are, as yet, largely unexplored. We will have more to say about the effects of training in the next chapter when we explore the training needed to hear changes in arbitrary backgrounds. But, as a generality, we must admit that little effort has been directed to this important area. Whether there are really different types of observers or simply differences in past listening experience remains a fascinating, but unsettled, question.

6
Training and Dynamic Effects

In this chapter, we take up two different and largely unrelated topics. The first is how the standard profile is learned. Detecting a change in a spectrum implies that some representation of the original spectrum exists, so that the change can be noted. Presumably, this representation of the original or "standard" spectrum must be established through some prior listening experience. Although we have discussed the need for extensive training of observers in profile experiments, we have not discussed the specifics of such training; for example, how many practice trials are required to reach asymptotic performance levels, or how the regularity of the standard spectrum affects the amount of training that is required to reach such asymptotes. We will do so here, as we review the only systematic study presently available on the topic. Next, we will consider an experiment in which the listener tries to detect a small intensity increment in one part of the spectrum while another part of the spectrum is used as an intensity comparison. The second spectral region can serve as a cue because both regions are changing in intensity in a correlated manner. These experiments may have some relevance to profile experiments, because both apparently require the listener to make simultaneous comparisons of the intensity level at different spectral regions. The obvious difference is that the spectrum is stationary in the case of profile experiments, whereas, in these new experiments, the intensity changes are dynamic. Because this change in intensity is produced by multiplying the two spectral regions by the same, slowly changing, waveform, the experiments are called "co-modulation experiments." As yet, only a few experiments have been conducted on this very interesting topic, but we will review those that are available.

TRAINING AND PROFILE ANALYSIS

In any profile experiment, one can think of the detection task as the discrimination of a change in some standard sound that serves as a reference stimulus. The signal may be regarded as some change, usually small, in that standard sound. Obviously, we must provide the observer with some experience with the standard so that the listener can learn how to recognize changes in this standard. In this section, we will discuss the training process and how quickly it can be accomplished. Admittedly, this is not a favorite topic for psychoacoustic studies. Traditionally, psychoacoustics has been concerned with how some stimulus variables affect detection performance, not how that detection level changes over time. Hafter and Carrier (1970) is a notable exception to this generalization. But, usually, we attempt to train the observer until asymptotic performance levels have been reached and then report only the performance levels at these asymptotic values. The following experiment will attempt to estimate the time required to reach asymptotic performance levels in typical profile analysis conditions. In the ensuing section, we will discuss some stimulus variables that affect such learning.

The regular profile standard

We often use a "regular" multicomponent complex as the standard stimulus in our profile task. The components of this complex are all equal in amplitude, and the frequency ratio between successive stimuli is constant; that is, the components are all equally spaced on a logarithmic frequency scale. One reason for using this regular complex, having equal-amplitude components and equal logarithmic frequency spacing, is that the basilar membrane can be thought of as a linear array where the position corresponding to the point of maximum vibration amplitude is roughly proportional to logarithmic frequency. Thus, our regular multicomponent complex will produce roughly equal excitation at nearly equal spatial intervals along this linear array.

Kidd, Mason, and Green (1986) have published data on the detection of an increment in the central component of such a complex sound as a function of the number of training trials. The standard consisted of 21 components with frequencies ranging from 300 to 3000 Hz. The central component of the complex was the 948-Hz component. The signal was an increment in the intensity of this central component. An adaptive procedure was used to estimate this threshold value using a 2-down 1-up rule. The duration of the stimulus was 100 msec. The median level of each component of the complex was 45 dB SPL, and the overall intensity was randomly varied over a 40-dB range. The signal threshold was estimated in the usual way, as the size of a component which, when added in phase to the background component, was detectable 71% of the time in the two-alternative forced-choice task.

Figure 6-1 shows the size of this signal component at threshold as a function of the number of listening trials in this detection task for a group of eight "naive" listeners. They were naive in the sense that, although some had previous experience in psychophysical listening tasks, none had listened in a "profile" experiment. Those with no previous listening

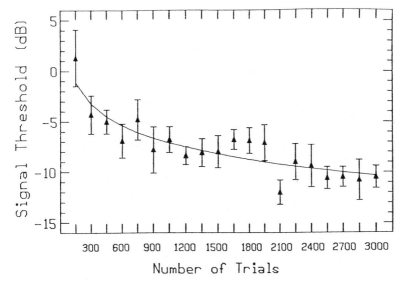

Figure 6-1. Avearge learning curve for a group of eight unpracticed listeners. The standard was our "regular" 21-component complex. The signal was an increment in the central component. The threshold of the signal is given in decibels re the level of the components of the standard. (From Kidd et al., 1986.)

experience received some training on a pure-tone intensity discrimination task to acquaint them with how to push the buttons and the timing used in these tests. Fifty adaptive trials were run to estimate the threshold level. The mean of the threshold values for the eight observers and the standard error, over observers, is indicated for every 150 trials in the course of the training. About 1000 trials were conducted each day so the 3000 observations represent approximately three days of listening in this task. Reasonably constant levels of performance were obtained after about 2500 trials. The solid curve fitted to the data is a logarithmic curve with the following parameters.

$$\text{Signal level} = -7.1 \log (N) + 14 \qquad \text{Eq. 6.1}$$

Thus, after about 100 trials, the threshold decreases about 2 dB for each double in the number of trials. The final level of performance obtained from these eight naive subjects is not particularly good and would probably improve with further practice. A more typical value for well-practiced observers (see Figure 4-1 or Figure 5-3) is in the −14 to −16 dB range rather than the value of −11 dB shown in Figure 6-1. Simple extrapolation of our logarithmic function would suggest that this level could be achieved if the amount of training were increased from 3000 to 12,000 trials. Although this value is probably near the amount of training required to reach asymptote, the formula should not be taken seriously because our approximation shows no asymptotic limit. Rather, it must be regarded as a reasonably good approximation to the data displayed in Figure 6-1.

The non-regular profile standards

Irregular frequency spacing

We believe the "regular" multicomponent standard is a particularly easy stimulus to learn as a reference in a profile experiment. Other, nonregular stimuli could also be used, but training would obviously be needed to teach the observer these other standard stimuli. We will now present the limited data we have on the ability of subjects to learn these nonregular standards and the asymptotic performance levels obtained with these stimuli. One way to produce a nonregular standard is to relax the restriction of placing successive components at the same frequency ratio. Ten standard stimuli were constructed using an 11-component complex, with all components equal in amplitude. The frequency of one component was 948 Hz and the signal, an increment in intensity, was added to that component. The remaining ten components of the standard were selected by drawing their frequencies from a set of 200 potential frequencies. These 200 frequencies were all equally spaced in logarithmic frequency in the range 300 to 3000 Hz. Such a selection procedure may yield a number of components whose frequencies are near the signal frequency and, hence, additional masking may result. To ameliorate the effects of masking to some degree, the component of the standard at the signal frequency, 948 Hz, was increased in amplitude by 6 dB. We have already seen that such a small pedestal at the signal frequency in an otherwise flat spectrum affects detection performance very little (see Figure 5-4).

The ten standard spectra produced by this procedure are illustrated in Figure 6-2. The value indicated with each panel is the average threshold obtained for that stimulus. This threshold is the decibel value of the signal amplitude re the amplitude of the standard component at this frequency. The average is based on the threshold obtained from four observers. These observers all participated in the experiment whose data are shown in Figure 6-1. The threshold value for each observer is based on 6 runs of 50 adaptive trials. The range of average thresholds for these non-regular standards is considerable, from -3.8 to -13.5 dB. A regular 11-component complex would produce a threshold in the -11- to -12-dB range.

An important question is whether these differences in thresholds are stimulus dependent or training dependent. Are the differences in threshold caused by differences among the placement in frequency of the components of the standard, or do some placements simply slow the learning process? In essence, we wish to know whether the asymptotic thresholds

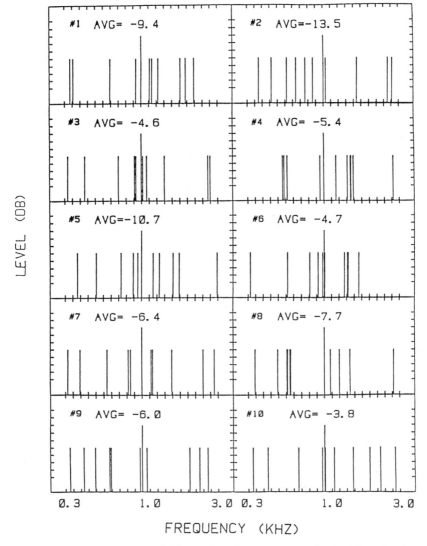

Figure 6-2. The spectra of 10 random-frequency standards. The signal was always an increment to the component whose frequency was 948 Hz. This level of that component was 6 dB higher than the other 10 components of the standard. The values given in the panels are the average thresholds for the particular standard. (From Kidd et al., 1986.)

would show the same pattern of results seen in Figure 6-1. To investigate this issue, we selected another set of ten standard spectra, using the same random procedure that we described above, and ran 1800 trials listening to each of the ten stimuli. The average threshold for the first 300 observations ranged from −4.8 to 11.3 dB, the mean over the ten stimuli was

−7.6 dB with a standard deviation of 2.4 dB. The thresholds for all ten stimuli improved as the number of listening trials increased; the average threshold for the last 300 trials was −11.6, a 5-dB improvement, with a standard deviation of 2.0 dB. The correlation between the threshold for the first and the last 300 trials was 0.91. Thus, the different standards produce real differences in threshold that apparently remain much the same with increases in training. More training on any of these stimuli will improve the ability to detect a change in the spectrum, but the relative rankings of the thresholds will stay much the same.

The next obvious question is: What are the stimulus factors that explain these differences in thresholds? An obvious candidate is simple masking. Perhaps the increment in some standards is more difficult to hear because, by virtue of the frequency placement of the components, there is more energy in the vicinity of the signal frequency. Clearly, in a general sense, masking could be an important process in determining the ability to hear a change in the spectrum. The question is whether this factor can explain the differences in threshold seen among the twenty random frequency component standards that we have just investigated. Kidd et al. (1986) investigated this issue in some detail in the original paper and they were unable to adduce any evidence to support the simple masking explanation. As with other profile experiments, it does not appear that stimulus factors in a local region of frequency about the signal play a very important role in the detection of the change in the spectrum. We still have no quantitative theory of why the different standards produce such different thresholds. But theories based on the entire distribution of the components in the standard, rather than those focused on the region of frequency near the signal, would appear to be more likely to produce accurate predictions.

Irregular intensity patterns

The subjects were the same ones whose data were reported earlier in this chapter. The standard stimulus was a 21-component complex (300 to 3000 Hz) with a frequency ratio of 1.12 between successive components. The signal was an increment in the central 948-Hz component. The irregularity of the standard was produced by varying the amplitudes of the components of the complex. This was accomplished by choosing the decibel value of each component's amplitude from a Gaussian or normal distribution with mean zero and standard deviation, sig_b. The signal component was always assigned the mean value (0 db). The overall level of the standard varied over a 40-dB range with the signal component having a median level of 45 dB SPL. The variability of the standard, sig_b, was varied in 2-dB steps, from 0 to 10 dB. For each level of variability, six different standard waveforms were constructed and tested. The average threshold, over subjects, for each of these six different standard stimuli is presented in Figure 6-3.

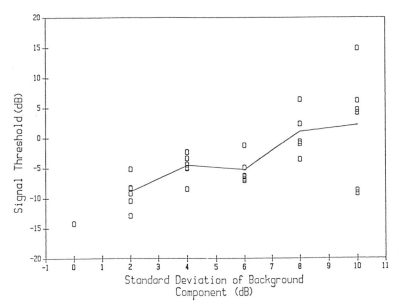

Figure 6-3. Average threshold for a group of standard waveforms whose components are regularly spaced in logarithmic frequency but whose amplitudes are randomly chosen. The signal was an increment in the central component of the 21-component complex. The amplitudes of the 20 nonsignal components were chosen from a Gaussian distribution of levels, with the same mean as the signal component and a standard deviation whose value is indicated along the abscissa. The thresholds for the different points plotted at any value of the abscissa are obtained from different standard waveforms composed of different random selections of amplitudes. (From Kidd et al., 1986.)

When sig_b is zero, the standard spectra is our regular standard with equal amplitude for all the components and equal logarithmic frequency spacing. The threshold is −15 dB when measured in terms of our usual signal amplitude re standard component level. With a relatively small, 2 dB, standard deviation among the components of the standard, the threshold is elevated some 5 dB on average, although the threshold for some of these stimuli with the irregular amplitudes is not much different from our regular standard stimuli. One should understand that these irregular stimuli were fixed for a block of trials, and the threshold for each of these six different standards was estimated from about 6 runs of 50 trials each (300 trials total). During that time, the observer is learning this new standard and further improvement in threshold might be expected if the trials continued. Whether the threshold for a change in these irregular standards would ever be as low as that obtained with the regular standard is not known. Probably some of the standard stimuli would improve to the −15 dB level with practice, but others, for the reasons we discuss later, probably would not. In any case, the variability in the thresholds obtained with these different standards is noteworthy. With a standard deviation of 10 dB, for example, some of the standard stimuli produce thresholds of nearly -10 dB, only about 5 dB above that produced by the regular standard. The *average* threshold value of these six stimuli with large amplitude variation, however, is almost $+2$ dB, about 17 dB worse than the threshold obtained with our regular profile standard.

One of these highly variable standards produced a threshold of $+15$dB. That value is clearly much higher than it should be. With a 40-dB randomization of overall level, it is possible to obtain a threshold of $+5$ dB by simply basing one's decisions on overall level (see Chapter 1, Appendix A, especially Figure 1-4). Once more, the observers appear to persevere on a detection procedure that is not optimum for a particular task. Again, this perseverance is understandable, since it occurs within a set of many conditions where listening for a relative change in level among components, rather than changes in overall loudness, is rewarded. Undoubtedly, extensive training on that single condition would lead to a change in behavior and, ultimately, a lower threshold. In any case, it is apparent that as the variability among the amplitudes of components of the standard increases, the threshold for an increment in the central component of the standard also increases.

The similarity of this experiment and the pedestal experiment discussed in the preceding chapter should be noted. As a rough rule of thumb, the total range of a set of values drawn from a normal distribution is about 4 to 6 times the standard deviation. Thus, with a sigma of 4 or 6 dB, the individual components of the standard stimulus may range over a 16- to 36-dB interval. Detecting a change in the spectrum of such a varied set of components is likely to be more difficult than detecting the same change in a set of equal-amplitude components, no matter how extensive the training. Recall that with the pedestal experiments, comparisons of components more than about 15 dB different in level were not handled as efficiently as the assessment of more modest intensity changes. Although some of the differences between these stimuli may be lessened by more extensive training, some of the differences will probably remain no matter how extensive the training.

CO-MODULATION RELEASE FROM MASKING

In all the preceding discussion of profile analysis, the standard spectrum was altered by changing the intensity at some region of the spectrum. To detect this change, the listener must simultaneously compare two different spectral regions. They must have had, therefore, some memory or representation of the standard spectrum in order to determine whether this comparison was indicative of the standard stimulus or the altered standard. We have just concluded a discussion of how much training is needed to establish such standards and how the composition of the standard affects the amount and extent of training that is needed to detect these alterations of the standard. Thus far, all the spectra we have discussed in this manuscript were stationary; the components were fixed in amplitude for the duration of the entire observation interval. In 1984, Hall, Haggard, and Fernandes reported on some threshold measurements with nonstationary spectra. These measurements are extremely interesting because they suggest that the simultaneous comparison can be carried out with stimuli that slowly change in average amplitude over time. In their experiments, it would appear that little, if any, training is necessary. These studies are recent and, although we do not have extensive information about this topic, they deserve careful consideration because they illuminate another facet of the spectral comparison process.

Let us begin with the first reported experiment (Hall, Haggard, & Fernandes, 1984). Basically, part of their experiment was a replication of Fletcher's classical critical band experiment (Fletcher, 1940). The threshold for a signal, in this case a 1000-Hz sinusoid, was measured as a function of the bandwidth of a masking noise centered about the signal. The usual results were found; the threshold for the signal increased as a function of noise bandwidth until a bandwidth of about 120 Hz was reached and then the threshold for the signal was independent of noise bandwidth. The break in this function allows one to estimate a "critical bandwidth" for the auditory system. In their data, the 3-dB estimate was about 80 Hz, a result similar to that obtained in numerous other studies of this topic (Swets, Green, & Tanner, 1962). This replication of Fletcher's experiment was essentially a control condition.

The important results were obtained in the experimental condition in which a small change was made in the dynamics of the masking stimulus. The critical change is that the masking noise was multiplied by another slowly varying noise. This second noise occupied a band of frequencies extending from 0 to 50 Hz. The resulting masking noise has the same average power as the masking noise used in the first control experiment, but its level slowly changes with time. Throughout the spectrum, the level of the noise slowly changes over time and these changes are obviously correlated because they are produced by the same multiplicative noise source. If one filtered the resulting noise in two separate bands, the outputs of these bands would be correlated random variables. A large output in one band would indicate that a large output in the other band is likely. The amount of this correlation would depend on the bandwidth of the noise bands that are sampled, since the stability of an estimate of noise level depends on the bandwidth and duration of the sample, as we discussed earlier (see Chapter 3, especially the section titled Noise Level Fluctuations).

Thus, in the experimental condition, Hall et al. repeated the traditional critical-band experiment using this special masking noise that varied slowly in level. The observer's task was still to detect a sinusoidal signal in the middle of this noise band. As the bandwidth of the masking noise was varied, the following results were obtained. At very small bandwidths, the thresholds were nearly the same as those obtained in the traditional experiment. As the bandwidth of the noise increased, the threshold for the signal decreased and at the wider bandwidth the signal was nearly 10 dB easier to hear with the nonstationary noise than with the stationary noise.

The improved detectability of the signal is undoubtedly attributable to the correlation between the sound level in the signal band and other, adjacent, frequency bands. In effect, the observer could be using two critical bands. One band is centered at the signal frequency. The second band is centered at some other frequency region and its level is used to predict the level in the signal band. That this explanation is essentially correct is supported by the second experiment of Hall et al. in which composite bands of 100, 300, 500, or 700 Hz, all centered at 1000 Hz, were constructed. Each of these bands was constructed so that adjacent 100-Hz bands were either coherent or incoherent. Thus, the levels in adjacent 100-Hz bands were all correlated in the coherent case and uncorrelated in the incoherent condition. The threshold for a 1000-Hz signal presented in such noise was the same for the 100-Hz width. For all wider bandwidths, the thresholds were about 5 to 6 dB different, with the coherent condition producing lower thresholds than the incoherent condition. Again, the results can be understood if one assumes that the ability to monitor two different critical bands, whose levels are correlated, improves the detection of a signal in one of the critical bands.

In a final and related experiment, two 100-Hz noise bands were used. One was centered at 1000 Hz and the observer was trying to detect a sinusoidal signal added to the band. We will call this noise band the "masker" band. The second noise band was also 100-Hz wide, but was located at some different center frequency. We will call this second noise band the "cue" band. The cue band was located both above or below the signal band in frequency and was centered 300, 200, or 100 Hz away from the masker band which was located at 1000 Hz. These cue bands were either correlated or uncorrelated with the masker band. As one might expect, the signal was easier to detect, by 3 to 5 dB, when the noise in the cue band is coherent with the noise centered at the signal frequency. Further, the amount of improvement was roughly the same whether the second band was located above or below the frequency of the signal band. There is some suggestion that the most improvement occurs when the cue band is close in frequency to the masker band, that is, the 100-Hz separation produces a somewhat greater co-modulation result than the 300-Hz separation.

In a more recent study, Hall (1985) has investigated the effects of difference in level between the masker band and the cue band. In that experiment, the signal was again a 1000-Hz sinusoid presented in a band of noise 100 Hz wide centered on the signal frequency. Two flanking bands served as the cue bands. One was located from 100 to 600 Hz and the second was situated from 1400 to 1900 Hz. These bands were either correlated or uncorrelated with the masker band. The independent variable of this experiment was the level difference between the masker and cue bands. In one experiment, the masker band was fixed at a spectrum level of 50 dB, and the level of the cue band was varied. In the second experiment, the cue band was fixed in level, again at 50 dB spectrum level, while the level of the masker band was varied. The results were similar in the two manipulations. If the cue and masker bands are nearly the same level, then the signal is easier to hear when the two bands are correlated rather than uncorrelated. This co-modulation effect, the difference between the threshold when the cue band was uncorrelated with the masker band minus the threshold when the cue band is correlated with the masker band, was about 5 dB. This effect diminishes when the masker and cue bands are different in level. If the two bands differ in level by more than about 20 dB, then there is essentially no co-modulation effect. These results are reminiscent of the pedestal effects we discussed earlier. In detecting changes in the shapes of spectra that are stationary, we found that it was easiest to hear the change when the level of the signal components was no more than 15 dB different from the level of the components of the standard.

McFadden has also recently measured how difference in level between the cue and masker bands influences the co-modulation results. His co-modulation effect was nearly abolished when there was a difference of about 10 dB in level between the cue and masker bands. There are, however, several differences between the stimulus parameters used in Hall's experiment and those used by McFadden. To understand these differences and why such changes were made, we must first consider several results presented by Cohen and Schubert in what, at present, are still unpublished reports. Cohen and Schubert (1986) initiated a number of very interesting experiments. The first simply confirmed many of the effects previously reported by Hall et al. (1984). Probably the most noteworthy variation in that experimental series was a binaural condition. Cohen and Schubert placed the cue band in one ear and the masking band in the opposite ear. The signal was a 1000-Hz sinusoid added to the center of the masker band. This dichotic condition produced a co-modulation result (the threshold for the signal was smaller when the two bands were correlated) that is not very different from that obtained when both bands are presented to the same ear.

In another series of experiments, Cohen and Schubert established the importance of absolute level and signal frequency on the size of the co-modulation result. In these experiments, the masker band and cue band were both 100 Hz wide. These two bands were equal in level and located next to each other in frequency. In one experiment, the absolute level of the two bands was varied. The masker band was centered at 1000 Hz, which was the frequency of the signal. The cue band was either immediately above the masker band or immediately below it in frequency. In both cases, the size of the co-modulation effect appears to increase with level; when the cue band was below the masker band, the effect was clearest. It was about 5 dB in size at the lower levels, 35 dB SPL, and about 10 dB at the highest level, 75 dB SPL. In the second experimental series, the cue and masker bands varied in frequency from about 250 to 4000 Hz. The co-modulation effect again increased with increases in frequency. Once more the most dramatic increase occurred when the cue band was just below the masker band. In short, Cohen and Schubert's results suggest that the largest difference in threshold between the correlated and uncorrelated conditions occurs when the cue and masker bands are at high levels and high frequencies. Typical differences will be as large as 10 dB for these optimum conditions, rather than the 5 dB measured in the original studies.

McFadden (1986) used high-frequency noise bands and high levels for his study of the effects of differences in level between the cue and masker bands. He used a 3700-Hz masker band, and a single cue band was either slightly below or above this frequency, 3500 or 3900 Hz. The overall level of the masker band was 70 dB, and the cue band was varied in level from 75 to 50 dB. The co-modulation effect is largest when the cue band is 75 dB and is essentially gone when the cue band reaches a level of 50 dB. The co-modulation effect has a somewhat smaller tolerance for a difference in level of the cue and masker bands than that claimed by Hall. This result is an important one because in any practical application of this co-modulation effect, for example, the perception of complex stimuli such as speech, it is unlikely that the levels in different frequency regions will be exactly the same. The available evidence suggests that level differences are not as critical at low as at high frequencies.

McFadden (1986) has also contributed to our understanding of how stimulus variables influence the size of the co-modulation results. He varied the duration of the signal from 75 to 375 msec. The masker or cue bands were, essentially, continuously present. The signal threshold was nearly constant in energy terms (time-intensity trade) for both the correlated and uncorrelated conditions. Thus, the size of the co-modulation effect was nearly the same at all durations. In a second experiment, McFadden varied the total presentation duration, that is, the signal and noise bands were all presented simultaneously. Once more, the size of the co-modulation effects was largely independent of duration, from 75 to 600 msec, although the greatest difference occurred at 375 msec.

In probably the most interesting experimental manipulation, McFadden varied the exact temporal alignment of the cue and masking bands. He did this by delaying the time waveform used to multiply the cue band. Varying this delay displaces the envelope of the cue band with respect to the masker band. Presumably, the correlation of the envelope is the essential information used to achieve the co-modulation result. The results for a 100-Hz band show that the size of the co-modulation effect diminishes from about 10 dB at zero delay to a value of about 3 dB at 3 msec delay. Delays greater than about 6 msec produce very small but measurable effect; beyond 10–12 msec there is essentially no co-modulation effect. Also, the data failed to show any cyclic effect at the period of the envelope. In general, the data show that the co-modulation results are extremely sensitive to rather small temporal delays between the envelopes of the two noise bands.

These results are extremely interesting and raise a number of empirical and theoretical questions that have yet to be answered. One simple question is whether we must use noise as the modulating waveform to produce the effect. Presumably, one could modulate the envelope in a sinusoidal manner and achieve some improvement in signal threshold when the envelope frequencies were the same as opposed to different. Also, if one added a DC to the sinusoidal modulator, one could determine how the degree of modulation influences the size of the co-modulation effect. One could also use the same frequency for each modulation waveform and vary the phase between the two signals. One can achieve coherence between two noise bands, but the level in cue band could vary inversely with the level in the other masker band. Will an improvement in the signal threshold still be achieved, or must the correlation between the two bands be positive in sign? Hall and his co-authors discuss their results in terms of the model of equalization and cancellation suggested by Durlach (1963). Durlach's model is used to account for the lower thresholds found in binaural experiments in which the signal is present in noise in one ear and the other ear contains the same correlated noise, but no signal. In effect, the noise in the second ear can serve as a cue, just as the second noise band serves as a cue in the co-modulation experiment. In the binaural experiments, the sign of the noise in the other ear is largely irrelevant. To a first approximation, both antiphasic and homophasic noises produce equal masking-level difference, the name given to this binaural effect. What would happen in the co-modulation experiment if the two bands, the masker and cue bands, were negatively correlated instead of positively correlated?

Another potential set of experiments should explore how fast this dynamic cue can operate. The rate at which the noise varies in level is determined by the bandwidth of the modulation noise. We know that co-modulation results can be obtained with multiplying noise that occupies a 50-Hz bandwidth, but how does the effect change as we increase or decrease the bandwidth of that noise? Presumably, with very large bandwidths for the multiplicative noise, the level fluctuations are so rapid that the cueing properties of the noise are lost.

Undoubtedly, the effects of the bandwidth of the multiplying noise will interact with the bandwidth of the resulting masking noise. The power level in the cueing band must be estimated in order to predict the level in the signal band. The stability of this estimate is determined by the bandwidth and duration of the cueing band in the way we have discussed (see Chapter 3). As the bandwidth of the cueing band increases, better and better estimates of the noise level should be possible. Indeed, there is some suggestion of the importance of this variable in the existing studies. Effects of 10 dB or so are common when the bandwidths of the cueing band are 500 to 1000 Hz; smaller effects are evident when the cueing band is only 100 Hz wide.

The question of noise fluctuations raises still another issue. Can the co-modulation effect be achieved with nonrandom maskers such as sinusoidal maskers? If predictable waveforms such as sinusoidal maskers were used in the experiments, would the size of the co-modulation effect be larger, because the estimated temporal varying levels could be made with better precision? Buus (1985) has recently published some data comparing the upper spread of masking produced by a single low-frequency sinusoid and a pair of sinusoids. The signal is a much higher frequency sinusoid, one or two octaves above the frequency region of the masker(s). As the frequency difference between the pair of maskers is varied, the amount of masking changes as one would expect. Since both components of the pair are equal in amplitude, the amplitude of the best pattern produced by their combination ranges between zero and twice the amplitude of either single component. When the pair of maskers is close in frequency, therefore, little masking is produced by the pair, since, in effect, the signal can be heard during a near-silent interval in the beat pattern. At frequency separations of 300 Hz and high intensity levels, however, a pair of sinusoidal maskers is still less effective than a single sinusoid of equal energy (by about 10 dB). This implies that rapid fluctuations in intensity level (as brief as 3 msec) can be used to overcome the effects of masking. This result strongly suggests that nonrandom maskers will also produce effects similar to those produced by noise maskers in co-modulation experiments.

But many more experimental results will need to be obtained before we have a very clear picture of the co-modulation mechanism. The answers to questions such as those discussed above will provide some of the background needed to formulate reasonable hypotheses about the nature of the co-modulation mechanism. It will also allow us to compare the results obtained with stationary spectra, such as those discussed in the bulk of the monograph, with dynamic stimuli such as those used in co-modulation experiments. At present, one can only guess at what aspects of the two areas are similar or different.

7

Two Theories of Profile Analysis

In the final chapter, we turn our attention from empiricism to theory. Ultimately, we will need to construct a theory of how the auditory system is able to detect changes in the shape of the acoustic spectrum. Many of the properties that describe how we hear a change in spectral shape are different and distinct from those studied in more traditional intensity-discrimination experiments. We hope the evidence reviewed in the preceding chapter has convinced the reader that a simple extension of the traditional theories of intensity discrimination is not adequate to explain how we detect spectral change. A theory of spectral shape detection must incorporate some new and different detection processes.

Many practical applications might benefit from such theory. Bucklein (1981) has published the results of a number of tests on the ability of observers to hear irregularities in the transfer functions of electroacoustic systems. The experiment should be credited as among the first experiments in auditory profile analysis, although he did not randomize the intensity of the two presentations in his paired-comparison tests. The need for theory is apparent in his paper. The only general conclusion of his study is that peaks in a spectrum are easier to hear than valleys, and that one must particularly eschew very narrow peaks.

In my opinion, it is still somewhat premature to begin this effort at theory construction. Many aspects of the process of discriminating a change in spectral shape are either unknown or for which we have only the most preliminary data. Given this ignorance, there are many ways the system might be constructed and insufficient data to suggest a clear choice of one formulation over an equally plausible, yet functionally distinct, alternative formulation. But, if relative ignorance were a sufficient reason for delaying theory construction, then few theories would ever be constructed. A theory does not need to be correct to be useful. Even incorrect theories suggest experiments that illuminate aspects of the process that would probably not be discovered without the theory. Also, the construction of a theory focuses one's attention on particulars and details of the process. It therefore clarifies our thoughts on exactly how the putative mechanism is supposed to operate and inevitably leads to the elimination of at least some alternatives. Thus, trying to construct a theory of profile analysis is likely to have several benefits aside from whether or not it accomplishes its major purpose, which is to correctly predict empirical facts.

Two theoretical frameworks

Two very recent developments will be the focus of this chapter. One, by Durlach, Braida, and Ito (1986) at the Research Laboratory of Electronics at MIT, is an outline for a theory for discriminating changes in what they call "broadband" signals. The theory is preliminary and presently is very general in nature. Nevertheless, it provides a concrete framework for approaching such discrimination processes and can later be modified by more specific assumptions as new data become available. I find the theory particularly appealing because it is an optimum theory. Given the limited information assumed to be available to the sensory system, one attempts to make optimum use of that information in detecting the signal. Thus, it shares with signal detection theory the assumption that the human observer tries to optimize the detection process within the constraints set by the data-acquisition process. The optimizing assumption provides a general way for a theory to predict how the observer will perform in a variety of different detection situations.

The MIT model is a "channel" theory. It begins with a linear filter bank. The incoming auditory signal is assumed to be analyzed in independent channels or filters. Although the width of these filters is not specified, presumably they are relatively narrow, perhaps the size of the critical band, roughly 10 to 15% of the center frequency of the filter. Waveform phase, insofar as it affects different channels, is lost at this early stage. This major theoretical assumption nicely incorporates a major empirical finding concerning the effects of waveform phase (see Chapter 4). The peripheral stage of the model is, therefore, similar to a number of other current models of the intensity-discrimination process that we called excitation models in Chapter 2; for example, the theories of Zwicker (1958), Whitfield (1967), and Florentine and Buss (1981). All these models assume that only the power spectrum of the stimulus is important.

The second theory we will consider is quite different in that it emphasizes much broader spectral regions than the channels discussed above. Also the computations of the second theory are sensitive to waveshape, that is, they are phase sensitive. It was not developed as a theory of profile analysis; rather, it was developed more than a decade ago by Larry Feth to account for pitch changes heard in relatively simple two-tone spectra (Feth, 1974). It has been refined and extended to a variety of experimental situations by Feth and his colleagues at the University of Kansas. When applied to profile experiments it represents an interesting contrast to the theories proposed by the MIT group. Feth's theory emphasizes what is apparent if one listens to these complex stimuli; namely, the change in spectral shape often produces a noticeable change in the pitch of the stimuli. The theory attempts to quantify these apparent pitch changes as scalar quantities, what they call the envelope weighted average instantaneous frequency (EWAIF) of the complex spectrum. Although Feth has demonstrated the utility of this theory in several simpler situations, there is little research on the application of these ideas to more complicated, relatively broadband spectra. We will briefly describe this approach at the conclusion of the chapter. These ideas deserve discussion if for no other reason than to provide an alternative to the channel approach discussed in the main body of the chapter.

THE CHANNEL APPROACH

We begin with the channel model of the MIT group. The specifics of the theory can best be understood by reference to Figure 2-5. The incoming acoustic signal is first filtered to separate the energy into different frequency channels. The output of each filter is then transformed so that an estimate of pressure level is obtained from each channel. This level estimate involves a nonlinear process and some temporal integration. This estimate of sound-pressure level is then assumed to be corrupted by some internal, Gaussian noise. This noise can be treated as if it were linearly combined with the level estimate. The model in this form has a particularly simple structure and can be applied to a variety of simple detection problems.

Discriminating a change in intensity level

Let us begin our description of the theory by applying it to the problem of detecting a change in the intensity of a broadband signal. We will refer to this detection problem as detecting a change in level or the "level-detection problem." We assume the signal is deterministic and, therefore, introduces no variability in the output of each channel. We will number the channels from 1 to n and denote a particular channel as Y_i. The internal noise at the output of each channel is independent of the output at all other channels and has some variance, σ_i. The mean output of the ith channel will be m_i when no increment is present and can be assumed to increase δ_i when the increment is added to the standard. The detection index or sensitivity parameter, d', for each individual channel can be summarized by the increase in the mean divided by the standard deviation,

$$d'_i = \Delta_i/\sigma_i \qquad \text{Eq. 7.1}$$

The combined d', because of the independence among the channels, is given by

$$d'_{comb} = \left[\sum_{i=1}^{n} (d_i)^2 \right]^{1/2} \qquad \text{Eq. 7.2}$$

which is the familiar vector combination rule (see Green & Swets, 1966, p. 239; also Green, 1958). Shortly, we will derive these two formulas in a more rigorous fashion.

Variance-covariance matrix

The assumption of independence between the channels is formally represented in the variance-covariance matrix, which lists the relationship between the outputs of the different channels in a row-column format (see Table 7-1). The entries of this matrix, for example, at the ith row and the jth column, are the covariance of the ith and jth columns, that is, the expected values of the cross product of two random variables. These random variables are proportional to the output of the ith and jth channels, but the means of each channel are subtracted before the cross product is computed (see the equation at the top of the table). The entry in the ith row and jth column can also be expressed as the product of $\rho\sigma_i\sigma_j$, where ρ is the covariance divided by the product of the standard deviation at the output of each channel (see bottom of the table). Usually ρ would be estimated as the Pearson correlation coefficient, r, computed in the usual way. For the minor diagonal entries, $i = j$, the correlation coefficient is unity and the σ are equal; therefore the entry is simply σ_i^2. Note that the matrix is symmetric about the minor diagonal, that is, the i,j entry and the j,i entry are the same.

For many detection problems, the matrix has a particularly simple form because the correlation coefficient between all different channels is zero ($\rho = 0$). All the off-diagonal entries of the matrix are then zero and the matrix only has entries along the diagonal, for example σ_i^2. We have

Table 7-1. General variance-covariance matrix, Σ; entries are $E(Y_i - m_i)(Y_j - m_j)$

$$\Sigma = \begin{bmatrix} \sigma_1^2 & \rho\sigma_1\sigma_2 & & & & \rho\sigma_1\sigma_n \\ \rho\sigma_2\sigma_1 & \sigma_2^2 & & & & \\ & & \cdot & & & \\ & & & \cdot & & \\ & & & & \cdot & \\ & & & & & \cdot \\ \rho\sigma_n\sigma_1 & & & & & \sigma_n^2 \end{bmatrix}$$

$$\rho = \frac{E(Y_i - m_i)(Y_j - m_j)}{\sigma_j\sigma_i} \qquad \sigma_i^2 = E(Y_i - m_i)^2$$

made one simplification in this presentation, since we have implicitly assumed that the matrix of intercorrelations is independent of which stimulus has been presented, either standard alone or standard plus increment. Thus, the entry in the ith, jth cell reflects only the sensory channels and not the stimuli presented to them. In the most general case, of course, one could have a matrix that was different for each potential stimulus condition.

Multivariate normal distribution

Because of the internal noise, there will be a distribution of different values at the output of each channel, even if the same deterministic stimulus is repeatedly presented. The distribution over the n channels will be a multivariate Gaussian distribution, since each individual channel is assumed to be Gaussian. The density function of that multivariate distribution has the following form.

$$f(\mathbf{Y}) = (2\pi)^{-n/2} \, |\Sigma|^{-1/2} e^{-1/2(\mathbf{Y}-\mathbf{m})\Sigma^{-1}(\mathbf{Y}-\mathbf{m})} \qquad \text{Eq. 7.3}$$

where $\mathbf{Y} = (Y_1, Y_2, \ldots, Y_n)$
$\quad \mathbf{m} = (m_1, m_2, \ldots, m_n)$
$\quad |\Sigma| = $ the determinant of Σ
$\quad \Sigma^{-1} = $ the inverse of Σ

where $\mathbf{Y}$ is the vector whose entries represent the outputs of the n channels. For those who have no background in matrix representation, van de Geer (1971) is recommended as a good introduction.

For the case we are considering, a change in level of a broadband signal, the channels are assumed to be independent, and therefore the variance-covariance matrix has nonzero entries only on the minor diagonal. The determinant of the variance-covariance matrix is then the product of the diagonal entries σ_i^2 and the square root of that product is the product of the standard deviations of each channel's output. The inverse of the variance-covariance matrix is the inverse of each element along the minor diagonal and the density function reduces to the following:

$$f(\mathbf{Y}) = \frac{1}{(2\pi)^{n/2}\sigma_1\sigma_2\cdots\sigma_n} \, e^{-\frac{1}{2}\left[\frac{Y_1-m_1}{\sigma_1}\right]^2\left[\frac{Y_2-m_2}{\sigma_2}\right]^2\cdots\left[\frac{Y_n-m_n}{\sigma_n}\right]^2} \qquad \text{Eq. 7.4}$$

or collecting the terms for each channel separately and expressing the density as a product of terms, we find

$$f(Y_1, Y_2, \cdots, Y_n)$$

$$= \frac{1}{\sqrt{2\pi\sigma_1^2}} \, e^{-\frac{1}{2}\left[\frac{Y_1-m_1}{\sigma_1}\right]^2} \frac{1}{\sqrt{2\pi\sigma_2^2}} \, e^{-\frac{1}{2}\left[\frac{Y_2-m_2}{\sigma_2}\right]^2} \cdots \qquad \text{Eq. 7.5}$$

$$\cdots \frac{1}{\sqrt{2\pi\sigma_n^2}} \, e^{-\frac{1}{2}\left[\frac{Y_n-m_n}{\sigma_n}\right]^2}$$

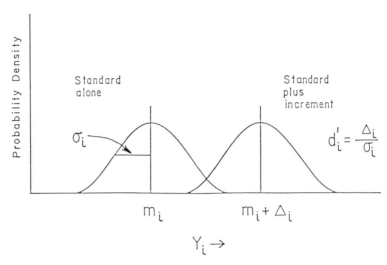

Figure 7-1.   The probability densities for the level at the output of a single channel. The mean, with standard alone, is m_i and is increased by Δ_i when the signal is added to the standard. The standard deviation of both distributions is σ_i.

The latter expression, the product form, is particularly revealing because it shows that the joint distribution is simply the product of the output of each channel, as it should be, since the channels are assumed to be independent. When the increment is added to the broadband signal, the mean output of each channel increases by an amount, Δ_i. There are, therefore, two multivariate densities. One is present when the standard alone is presented; in this case, the mean of each channel in the case is m_i. The other multivariate density is present when the increment is added to the standard; in this case, the mean of each channel is $m_i + \Delta_i$. Figure 7-1 shows the probability density of the ith channel for the two stimulus possibilities. The detectability of the increment on the ith channel is determined by the sensitivity index, d'_i, which is given in the figure as the increment in the mean divided by the standard deviation.

Likelihood ratio

To determine the detectability of the increment over all the channels, we assume the observer uses an optimum detection strategy and computes the likelihood ratio of the channel outputs given the two hypotheses, either standard alone or standard plus increment. We compute the likelihood ratio using the product form for the multivariate densities, Eq. 7.5, because the likelihood ratio then reduces to a product of terms of the following type.

$$\ell\,(Y_1 Y_2 \cdots Y_n) = \frac{f(Y_1 Y_2 \cdots Y_n \mid \text{standard plus increment})}{f(Y_1 Y_2 \qquad Y_n \mid \text{standard alone})} \qquad \text{Eq. 7.6}$$

$$\ell = \cfrac{\dfrac{1}{\sqrt{2\pi\sigma_1^2}}\, e^{-\frac{1}{2}\left[\frac{Y_1 - m_1 - \Delta_1}{\sigma_1}\right]^2} \cdots \dfrac{1}{\sqrt{2\pi\sigma_n^2}}\, e^{-\frac{1}{2}\left[\frac{Y_n - m_n - \Delta_n}{\sigma_n}\right]^2}}{\dfrac{1}{\sqrt{2\pi\sigma_1^2}}\, e^{-\frac{1}{2}\left[\frac{Y_1 - m_1}{\sigma_1}\right]^2} \cdots \dfrac{1}{\sqrt{2\pi\sigma_n^2}}\, e^{-\frac{1}{2}\left[\frac{Y_n - m_n}{\sigma_n}\right]^2}}$$

In this form, it is obvious that the likelihood ratio for the entire set of outputs is equal to the product of the likelihoods of the individual channels

$$\ell\,(\mathbf{Y}) = \ell\,(Y_2) \cdots \ell\,(Y_n)$$

where the likelihood for a single channel is

$$\ell\,(Y_i) = \cfrac{\dfrac{1}{\sqrt{2\pi\sigma_i^2}}\, e^{-\frac{1}{2}\left[\frac{Y_i - m_i - \Delta_i}{\sigma_i}\right]^2}}{\dfrac{1}{\sqrt{2\pi\sigma_i^2}}\, e^{-\frac{1}{2}\left[\frac{Y_i - m_i}{\sigma_i}\right]^2}}$$

$$\ell\,(Y_i) = e^{+\frac{\Delta_i}{\sigma_i}\left[\frac{Y_i - m_i}{\sigma_i}\right] - \frac{1}{2}\left[\frac{\Delta_i}{\sigma_i}\right]^2} \qquad \text{Eq. 7.7}$$

The logarithm of the likelihood ratio is, obviously, monotonic with the likelihood ratio and is a convenient transformation at this point, because it reduces the product of likelihoods to a sum of logarithmic terms (see Eq. 7.6) and each term of the sum has the following form:

$$\ln \ell\,(Y_i) = Z_i + c_i \qquad \text{Eq. 7.8}$$

$$Z_i = \frac{\Delta_i}{\sigma_i}\left[\frac{Y_i - m_i}{\sigma_i}\right] \qquad c_i = -\frac{1}{2}\left[\frac{\Delta_i}{\sigma_i}\right]^2$$

From this equation, we want to compute the detectability index, both for each channel and for the combined channels.

The detectability index, d'

The constant term of Eq. 7.8 is unchanging and hence unimportant. What we would like is the distribution of the term, Z_i, which is proportional to the random variable, Y_i. Each term, Z_i, must be Gaussian, because it is a linear function of Y_i, itself a Gaussian random variable. The term within brackets is in standard form, with mean zero and variance one. This standardized variable is multiplied by the constant Δ_i/σ_i. If the stim-

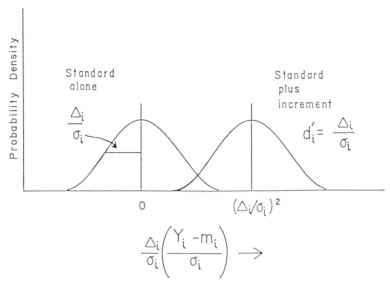

Figure 7-2.   The probability densities for a transform of the level at the output for a single channel. (See Eq. 7.8.) The mean of this variable is 0 when only the standard is present, and increases to the square of the common standard deviation. The d' value is equal to this standard deviation.

ulus condition is the standard alone, then the mean of Y_i is m_i. In that case, Z_i has mean zero and a variance equal to the square of the constant multiplier, Δ_i/σ_i. Similarly, if the stimulus condition is the standard plus an increment, then the mean of Y_i is $\Delta_i + m_i$ and the mean of Z_i is the square of Δ_i/σ_i. The variance is the same as before, namely, the square of Δ_i/σ_i. Figure 7-2 displays the two densities for each stimulus condition. The expression for the sensitivity index, d', is shown in the figure. It is simply the increase in the means produced by the increment divided by the common standard deviation.

The combined logarithm for the likelihood ratio for all the independent channels is a sum of the variables, Z_i, from the individual channels. This sum is Gaussian, because all the individual random variables in the sum are Gaussian. The combined mean is the sum of the individual means. Because the individual random variables are all independent, the combined variance is the sum of the individual variances. Thus, the combined sensitivity is

$$d'_{comb} = \frac{\sum_{i=1}^{n} \left(\frac{\Delta_i}{\sigma_i}\right)}{\left[\sum_{i=1}^{n} \left(\frac{\Delta_i}{\sigma_i}\right)^2\right]^{1/2}} = \left[\sum_{i=1}^{n} \left(\frac{\Delta_i}{\sigma_i}\right)^2\right]^{1/2} = \left[\sum_{i=1}^{n} (d_i)^2\right]^{1/2} \qquad \text{Eq. 7.9}$$

As we stated earlier, the combined d' value is merely the sum of squares of the d' values from the individual channels. This vector addition rule is a common result for detectors that make optimal use of independent (i.e., uncorrelated) sources of information.

Before continuing our mathematical derivations for the detector of a change in spectral shape, let us comment on the nature of the detector process for this case of a change in level of a deterministic signal. First, one should note that the detector must know the level of the channel output for the standard alone. The level on a given stimulus presentation is compared with this standard level, and the difference between them constitutes the basis for a decision among the stimulus alternatives. There must therefore be some memory process that acquires the level of the stimulus for the standard. Second, the channels themselves must be independent. Given a fixed stimulus condition, there is no correlation among the outputs of the various channels. This fact does not, however, preclude similar increases in several channels brought about by the stimulus. For example, an increment in the output of one channel might cause an increase in some neighboring channels. Such relations would be determined by the nature of the filtering occurring in the first stage filter bank, the character of the filter, and the specific stimuli. Excitation models, so called, assume that the presentation of an intense stimulus, such as a single sinusoid, will create increases in the outputs of many channels, especially those tuned to frequencies above the signal frequency. The channel with the greatest sensitivity—the one contributing the largest individual d'—may or may not be the channel tuned to the signal frequency. Nonlinear effects of various kinds may create greater sensitivity at some channel different from the one tuned to the signal frequency, so called "off-frequency" listening (Leshowitz & Wightman, 1971). Thus far, in our work, there has been little exploration of the effects of correlation among various channels. The independent model is the only version of this general, multivariate Gaussian model that has received much attention. Finally, the usual way to account for why detection performance is roughly constant for constant ratios of increment to standard (i.e., Weber's law) is to assume the noise is added to the channel output *after* the nonlinear transformation of the stimulus has been performed. For example, if level is estimated via a logarithmic transform of stimulus power, then Weber's law is immediately predicted. Departures from Weber's law could then be attributed to details of how the increments in various channels occur with change in stimulus level.

Discriminating a change in spectral shape

Let us now turn our attention to the detection of a change in spectral shape. Changes in shape can be represented as changes among the output levels over the various channels. We let m_{ki} be the mean level of the output of the ith channel [$i = 1 \cdot \cdot \cdot n$] when the kth stimulus [$k = 1,2$] is presented. For example, $k = 1$ would imply the standard alone was present, while $k = 2$ would imply the standard plus the signal was present. The difference in level at the ith channel is simply $\Delta_i = m_{2i} - m_{1i}$. Without a randomization of overall level, there is no important difference between detecting a change in spectral shape and detecting a change in level. We may regard the mean output, m_{1i}, as the standard stimulus and the change producing the new mean, m_{2i}. The change may be either an increase or decrease in the mean, but the sensitivities for each channel would be as before, and the combined sensitivity would be as given in Eq. 7.9.

Variance-covariance matrix

With random changes in overall level for each stimulus presentation, however, the situation is altered in a fundamental way. Randomizing the overall level obviously causes the output level in one channel to be correlated with the output level in a different channel. We will represent this common variation in output level assuming that we have a common random variable added to the output of each channel; we denote this random variable as ω. It is convenient to represent changes in ω as deviations from a mean value of zero, thus $E(\omega) = 0$. When there is random variation in overall level, the output of any channel is then the random variation inherent in each channel (and independent across channels) and a common variation ω. We present this total output of the ith channel as $Y_i + \omega$. The covariance between channels is

$$E(Y_i + \omega)(Y_j + \omega) = \sigma_\omega^2$$

because we assume the channels are independent of each other and of the random variable, ω; thus, $E(Y_i Y_j) = 0$ and $E(Y_i \omega) = 0$ for all i and j. Although experimentally we generally vary overall level in a rectangular fashion, it is convenient mathematically to assume that ω is Gaussian. If ω is Gaussian, then the distribution of the outputs of the channels, under either of the stimulus conditions, is still a multivariate normal but with a different variance-covariance matrix than we considered in the previous case. Now, each cell off the minor diagonal does have a nonzero entry, σ_ω^2. Also, the cells along the minor diagonal have a larger value; namely, the variance associated with the noise in that channel, η_j^2, and, in addition to that variance an additional variance, σ_ω^2, from the random changes in overall level.

We should pause at this point to comment on the relationship between the entries of Table 7-2 and those in the general variance-covariance matrix of Table 7-1. These relationships are simply a matter of definition, but it may clarify the presentation to carefully consider the entries in each table. In particular, it will be interesting to derive how the correlation between channels, ρ, depends on η and ω. Let us begin with the cells along

Table 7-2. Variance-covariance matrix for change
in spectral stage

$$\Sigma = \begin{bmatrix} \eta_1^2 + \sigma_\omega^2 & \sigma_\omega^2 & \sigma_\omega^2 \\ \sigma_\omega^2 & \eta_2^2 + \sigma_\omega^2 & \\ \sigma_\omega^2 & & \eta_n^2 + \sigma_\omega^2 \end{bmatrix}$$

the minor diagonal. In the general case (Table 7-1), the entry represents the variance of the ith channel. For the correlated case (Table 7-2), that entry represents the contributions of two terms. The first term in the sum is equal to the internal variance in the particular channel, η_i^2. To that variability is added a second term σ_ω^2, which arises because of correlation between the channels induced by changing the overall level of the stimulus on each presentation. Obviously, the amount of that variability can be altered by the experimenter, who could change it by changing the range of level variation used in a particular experiment. Let us also consider the case when the internal noise is equal across all channels; then, given these definitions, we have that $\eta^2 + \sigma_\omega^2$, for the correlated case, must be equal to σ^2 for the general case.

Let us now consider the off-diagonal entries. According to Table 7-1, the off-diagonal entries contain a correlation term, ρ, yet the off-diagonal term in Table 7-2 is equal to σ_ω^2. Because these matrices represent the same quantities in different notation we should be able to relate ρ to the two variances of the correlated case. Since the off-diagonal entries must be equal, we know that $\rho\sigma^2$ of Table 7-1 must equal σ_ω^2 of Table 7-2. Thus, substituting for σ^2, we conclude that ρ is equal to $\sigma_\omega^2/(\eta^2 + \sigma_\omega^2)$. The latter is an entirely reasonable result, because it asserts that the correlation between two noisy channels is the common variance divided by the total variance.

The detectability index

To write out the multivariate density for the channel output when the variance-covariance matrix is given by Table 7-2, we would have to find the inverse to this matrix and its determinant and use the appropriate values in Eq. 7.3. The MIT group has carried out these calculations and determined the sensitivity index for this case. We will simply quote their results here. According to Durlach, Braida, and Ito (1985), the combined d' over the n channels is

$$d' = \left[\sum_{i=1}^{n} \left(\frac{\Delta_i}{\eta_i} \right)^2 - \Omega \right]^{1/2} \qquad \text{Eq. 7.10}$$

where

$$\Omega = \frac{A\sigma_\omega^2}{A + \sigma_\omega^2} \left(\sum_{i=1}^{n} \frac{\Delta_i}{\eta_i^2} \right)^2$$

and

$$A = \left(\frac{1}{\eta_1^2} + \frac{1}{\eta_2^2} \cdot \cdot \cdot \frac{1}{\eta_n^2} \right)^{-1}$$

Note that this detectability index for the combined channels is composed of two terms. The first term within the brackets is the combined detectability index for our previous case (see Eq. 7.9). From this term, we subtract the term denoted Ω. This term is generally non-negative, so the first important prediction of this model is that detection of changes in spectral shape, if the overall stimulus level is randomized, will be poorer than when the overall level is fixed. This follows because without the random variation in level, the correlation between channels will be zero—if $\sigma_\omega = 0$, then the term Ω will be zero. We have already reviewed some evidence (see Chapter 5) where at least some observers performed better at detecting a change in spectral shape than a change in level of a single sinusoidal component. But in that experiment the level of the stimulus was fixed, so that, in principle, there was no reason to expect correlation between the channels. It is our general impression that randomizing the overall intensity level always leads to slightly poorer detection performance, but whether the amount of the difference can be predicted by this model is still a moot point.

Let us explore one more assumption before commenting more generally about the difference between the equation for detecting a change in shape and the detection of changes in level. Consider the case when the internal noise variance is the same for all channels—η_i is constant and independent of the channel number. In that case, certain simplifications can be carried out for the Ω term in Eq. 7.10. These simplifications result in the following formula:

$$d' = \left[\sum_{i=1}^{N} \left(\frac{\Delta_i}{\eta} \right)^2 - \frac{\sigma_\omega^2}{\eta^2 + N\sigma_\omega^2} \frac{1}{\eta^2} \left(\sum_{i=1}^{N} \Delta_i \right)^2 \right]^{1/2} \qquad \eta^2 = \eta_i^2 \text{ for all } i$$

Eq. 7.11

Again, the leading term within the bracket is the combined detectability index for detecting a simple change in level. The second term, which subtracts from the first, arises because of the correlation between the channels. For a finite number of channels, n, the second term will be zero in two cases. The first such case is if σ_ω is zero; that is, if there is no correlation between the channels. In that case, as we would expect, Eq. 7.11 is exactly equal to Eq. 7.9. A second way for these two equations to be the same is if the last term, the summation over the increments, Δ_i, is zero. Durlach, Braida, and Ito (1986) describe this condition as detecting two stimuli that are "balanced" because the sum of the increments over the channels is exactly equal to the sum of the decrements. There is very little data available on the detection of these balanced signals and practically none comparing detection performance of balanced and unbalanced signals.

In concluding our discussion of the channel models, let us consider a simple case of only two channels. We will derive the detection structure for this two-channel detector when faced with our two detection problems. In the first case, we are trying to detect a change in level. In the second, we are trying to detect a change in spectral shape. Differences in the kinds of information available in these two cases will lead to different structures for the detectors. In particular, as this simple example will illustrate, the outputs of the channels, Y_i, are treated in different ways in the two cases.

Bi-variate normal example

With only two channels, and with the assumption that the variance in each channel is the same, the bi-variate normal distribution can be written in the following way.

$$\frac{1}{2\pi\sigma^2 (1 - \rho^2)^{1/2}} e^{-\frac{1}{2(1 - \rho^2)}\left[\left(\frac{Y_1 - m_1}{\sigma}\right)^2 - \frac{2\rho(Y_1 - m_1)(Y_2 - m_2)}{\sigma^2} + \left(\frac{Y_2 - m_2}{\sigma}\right)^2\right]} \qquad \text{Eq. 7.12}$$

Now consider the detection of a change in level. In that case, the correlation between channels, ρ, is zero. The mean will be m_i if the standard alone is presented and $(m_i + \Delta_i)$ if the standard plus increment is presented. These assumptions are summarized in Table 7-3.

For the case of detection of a change in spectral shape, we assume that the overall level of the stimulus is a random variable. We also assume that the internal noise variance is the same in each channel. In that case, the value of the correlation, ρ, will have the value $\sigma_\omega^2/(\eta_i^2 + \sigma_\omega^2)$, as we dis-

Table 7-3. Parameters for two-channel detection

Change in Level	Standard Alone	Standard Plus Increment
m	m_i	$m_i + \Delta_i$
σ	σ_i	σ_i
ρ	0	0

Change in Spectral Shape

m	m_i	$m_i + \Delta_i$
σ	$\eta_i^2 + \sigma_\omega^2$	$\eta_i + \sigma_\omega^2$
ρ	$\dfrac{\sigma_\omega^2}{\eta_i^2 + \sigma_\omega^2}$	$\dfrac{\sigma_\omega^2}{\eta_i^2 + \sigma_\omega^2}$

cussed previously. The sigmas for each channel will be the same, namely, $\eta_i^2 + \sigma_\omega^2$, and the means will be as we discussed in the previous case, namely, m_i for one stimulus alternative and $m_i + \Delta_i$ in the other case. Again, these assumptions are summarized in Table 7-3.

It will simplify the remaining derivations if we assume that the means, m_i, are equal to zero. This can be done without loss of generality, since the exact value of the mean is unimportant—only the change in these values, Δ_i, is important. For a similar reason, we set the σ equal to unity. In that case, the likelihood ratio, for either detection problem, reduces to a simple form.

$$\log \ell \, (Y_1 Y_2) = -\frac{1}{2 \, (1 - \rho^2)} \{(Y_1 - \Delta_1)^2 - Y_1^2$$
$$- 2\rho \, [(Y_1 - \Delta_1) \, (Y_2 - \Delta_2) - Y_1 Y_2] \qquad \text{Eq. 7.13}$$
$$+ (Y_2 - \Delta_2)^2 - Y_2^2\}$$

If this equation is expanded, one will note that only some of the terms depend on the random variables Y_1 and Y_2; the rest of the terms are constant and can be ignored. Thus, one can show that the log of likelihood ratio is proportional to the following expression:

$$\log \ell \, (Y_1 Y_2) \propto Y_1 \, (\Delta_1 - \rho\Delta_2) + Y_2 \, (\Delta_2 - \rho\Delta_1) \qquad \text{Eq. 7.14}$$

This equation, in turn, can be considered for two cases. Case I is the level detection problem; in this case, $\rho = 0$ and the increments $\Delta_1 = \Delta_2$. For this case, the detector simply adds the output of the two channels and compares that sum with the expected levels for the standard-plus-increment or standard alone. This is the usual structure for the level detector and is what one might have expected. For Case II, the correlation between channels is nonzero; in fact, $\rho > 0$, because of the random variation in overall level. If the stimulus is balanced, then the increment on one channel is equal to the same increment on the other channel, except the signs are reversed, for example, $\Delta_1 = -\Delta_2$. In that case, the bracketed terms in Eq. 7.14 are simply opposite in sign; thus, the detector may simply subtract the output of the two channels and base its decision on that quantity. This will be an optimal decision strategy because this difference is proportional to the logarithm of likelihood ratio. If that difference of outputs is positive, then there is greater likelihood that the increment has been added to the standard. If the increment is minus, then there is greater likelihood that only the standard alone is present. Again, the general structure of the detector is what one might expect for a task involving the detection of a change in spectral shape.

The importance of this example lies in its illustration that the form of the detector depends on the details of the detection task and, in particular, on how the experimental task influences certain parameters of the detection process. The important difference in this example was whether or not the channel outputs were correlated. As we stated earlier, the MIT model is a general framework for analyzing such detection problems. More specific assumptions can and must be added to the model in addition to the very general assumptions about correlation or that lack of it discussed here. These assumptions will be based on new experimental evidence as it is forthcoming. In the concluding section of this chapter we consider an alternative approach—that suggested by Feth's EWAIF model.

FETH'S EWAIF MODEL

As we explained previously, Feth's EWAIF model is a theory of how a dynamically changing stimulus can be heard as a single pitch. Although it has previously been applied largely to two-tone stimuli, formally, there is nothing to prevent its application to much more complicated spectra such as our profile stimuli. Unlike the MIT model, Feth's EWAIF (envelope weighted average of the instantaneous frequency) model is not concerned with limited frequency channels, but assumes that the processing of complex auditory waveforms may occur over a relatively wide frequency range. In particular, the approach assumes that changing the relative amplitude of components in a complex spectrum may introduce a slight pitch change that is the basis for detecting the difference between the standard and the standard-plus-signal spectra. Whether or not this approach will be useful for multicomponent signals distributed over several octaves is uncertain. But its validity in analyzing certain situations is undeniable. These situations occur where the complex spectra consists of a few sinusoidal components and where the total range of frequencies covered by these components is less than a single octave. The model also provides an interesting contrast to the channel approach we have just considered. It is certainly prudent to know about this viewpoint, because Feth and his co-workers have clearly demonstrated its usefulness in certain detection situations.

To understand this model in more detail, we must begin by representing the waveform in a particular way. The following discussion borrows heavily from two articles by Voelcker (1966a, 1966b). The reader should consult these papers for a more detailed and more rigorous development. Let us represent the waveform, $f(t)$, a real function of time, in the following manner.

$$f(t) = e(t) \cos p(t) \qquad \text{Eq. 7.15}$$

where $e(t)$ and $p(t)$ are real functions called the instantaneous envelope and instantaneous phase angle. It is also usual to define a quantity called the instantaneous frequency, inst $f(t)$, in terms of the derivative of the instantaneous phase angle, thus

$$\text{inst } f(t) = \frac{1}{2\pi} \frac{dp(t)}{dt}$$

Clearly, such a representation of any realistic waveform is possible, since we have simply replaced a single waveform with two others. Consider a narrow-band process, such as a filtered noise waveform, then $e(t)$ would represent the relatively slow changing magnitude of the envelope and $p(t)$ could represent the center frequency of the noise, f_0, and some slow variation about that frequency. A phase modulated carrier frequency, F, can be written as

$$f(t) = A \sin [2\pi Ft + \theta(t)]$$

where A is the envelope, in this case a constant, and $\theta(t)$ is the variation in the phase of the carrier. Variation in this phase term changes the instantaneous frequency of the carrier, and for this case the instantaneous frequency is simply the time derivative of the term within brackets divided by 2π, or

$$F + \frac{1}{2\pi} \frac{d\theta(t)}{dt}$$

In general, the instantaneous frequency of a complex waveform varies over time but, nonetheless, the auditory system may appreciate such a complex wave as having a single, stationary pitch. For example, two equal-amplitude sinusoids of high frequency separated by a small frequency interval will be heard as a single sinusoid, wavering in amplitude but having a pitch equal to the mean frequency of the two components (see the discussion of Reisz's amplitude discrimination experiment in Chapter 3). Feth has proposed that the auditory system computes this stationary pitch value by calculating a weighted average of the instantaneous frequency, where the weighting function is the instantaneous envelope. Feth and his collaborators have demonstrated the utility of this approach for a variety of narrow band waveforms (Feth, 1974; Feth & O'Malley, 1977; Feth, O'Malley, & Ramsey, 1982; and Stover & Feth, 1983).

To apply these ideas generally, we need to have a calculation procedure that will produce the two functions, $e(t)$ and $p(t)$, the instantaneous envelope and phase terms of Eq. 7.15, so that we can calculate the instantaneous frequency [by differentiating $p(t)$] and performing the weighted frequency calculation, EWAIF. The straightforward way of carrying out these calculations is via the Hilbert transform (Cooper & McGillem, 1967). Let us denote the Hilbert transform of $f(t)$ and $H(t)$. As an expository device, it is convenient to consider an additional waveform, called the analytic waveform, $\hat{g}(t)$, which may be defined in a fashion analogous to a complex number, namely,

$$\hat{g}(t) = f(t) + jH(t)$$

where j is the imaginary number, $j = (-1)^{1/2}$. The advantage of this analytic signal is that the instantaneous envelope, $e(t)$, has a simple interpretation; it is the magnitude of the analytic signal $\hat{g}(t)$. Also, the instantaneous phase, $p(t)$, at any fixed time is simply the instantaneous angle of the complex number

$$e(t) = [f(t)^2 + H(t)^2]^{1/2}$$
$$p(t) = \tan^{-1} H(t)/f(t)$$

From $p(t)$, one can determine the instantaneous frequency, inst $f(t)$, by differentiating $p(t)$ and dividing by 2π. Thus, the value of EWAIF is

$$\text{EWAIF} = \frac{\int_0^T \text{inst } f(t) \, e(t) \, dt}{\int_0^T e(t) \, dt}$$

The interval of integration, T, deserves some discussion since it is, in principle, an important parameter of the auditory process. To date, the model has been applied almost exclusively to periodic stimuli, so that the period of integration is simply set to one period of the complex wave. In applying this theory generally, one will have to determine the time window over which this average is to be made. For the present, this is an unresolved question, although research is underway to investigate this issue (Feth, 1986). Let us now turn to the application of these ideas to profile analysis.

Applications of the EWAIF model

Consider the change in relative amplitude of the simplest possible profile stimulus, a two-component spectrum. Suppose the amplitudes of the two components are slightly different: either the higher-frequency component is slightly more intense than the lower-frequency component or the reverse. If the two tones are relatively close in frequency and the difference in amplitude is 1 dB, then subjects can discriminate the relative amplitudes of the two components (Feth & O'Malley, 1977). That is, subjects can discriminate the different amplitude profiles produced by the two component complex. The listeners report that they make the discrimination on the basis of differences in the pitch of the waveforms—the pitch is near the mean frequency but shifted slightly toward the more intense component. At relatively small frequency separations, the discrimination is very good, but as the frequency separation between the two components is increased, an upper frequency limit is reached where the discrimination begins to decline. The frequency width of this upper limit increases in roughly constant proportion to the center frequency of the complex. It is much wider than a critical band estimate, however, and appears to be a bit larger than half the center frequency of the complex. Presumably, at this wide a frequency separation, the two components no longer interact within a single filter of the auditory system and the ability to hear pitch changes in the complex is lost. Feth et al. (1982) have demonstrated that the pitches of these two-component complexes vary in the way one would expect from the EWAIF model and explore some of the stimulus parameters that affect such pitch matches.

A more recent application of this model has attempted to account for the discrimination of a change in the intensity of a central component (1000 Hz) of a multitonal complex as the number and density of the components in this waveform are varied. This is the experiment discussed in detail in Chapter 4 (see Figure 4-2). The interesting data for this model are the changes in threshold as the number of components in the complex was varied. When the number was altered from 3 to 11, holding the total frequency range constant, the ability to detect an increment in the central component improved some 14 dB. Frankly, this much improvement, as a function of number of components, is an embarrassment for the channel point of view. More components will stimulate more independent channels, but the simplest models would predict only square root improvements, or factors of $(11/3)^{1/2} = 1.9$ changes in d'.

According to the EWAIF model, we should compute the changes in average frequency produced by adding the increment to the central component of the complex. Thus, Feth computed an envelope weighted frequency for the standard waveform and for the waveform containing the standard plus increment, using the increment value indicated in the data of Figure 4-2. The changes in pitch caused by adding the increment to the standard were about 20 Hz for the three- and five-tone complexes and then increased for the greater number of components. Feth then considered how these quantities would be affected if he assumed the listener filtered the signal using the wide filter bandwidth suggested by his two-tone studies. Specifically, a 700 Hz-wide filter was centered at 1000 Hz and the envelope weighted average frequencies were again computed for the different experimental conditions. The frequency differences (frequency of the standard plus signal minus frequency of the standard) ranged between -10 and -20 Hz—remarkably constant pitch differences for a variety of experimental conditions with thresholds varying over a 14-dB range. As Feth and Stover (1987) say in summarizing these results, "it may be more reasonable to assume that [the listeners] are responding to pitch differences between equal-amplitude and incremented profile arrays rather than detecting an ever-smaller 'bump' on the line-spectrum representations of these complex sounds."

While it is premature to try to evaluate the ability of the EWAIF model to predict all the profile results, one important property of the model should be mentioned. The calculation procedure is not independent of relative phase of the components of the waveform. With a two-component complex, the most popular testing ground for this theory, the phase is obviously irrelevant. With more components, phase effects could be more important. With the logarithmic spacing used in many profile experiments, the phase effects are likely to be less important than in harmonic sequences. In any case, the average frequency calculated by this model for a general complex stimulus does depend on the relative phase of the components and this feature of the model should be kept in mind. The empirical evidence (see Chapter 4) suggests that relative phase is largely unimportant, but, as with all empirical results, we cannot prove that it plays no role whatsoever.

Whatever the ultimate role of the EWAIF model, it provides an interesting alternative to the limited channel model discussed earlier. As with most models, each may be effective in providing explanations of results obtained in particular stimulus situations. Both models are very new and the exploration of the full implications of these positions has only begun. We hope these discussions have revealed some of the issues that face any theorist trying to provide a comprehensive account of how the auditory system detects changes in the shape of complex acoustic spectra.

References

Anderson, D. J. (1973). Quantitative model for the effects of stimulus frequency upon synchronization of auditory nerve discharges. *Journal of the Acoustical Society of America, 54,* 361–364.

Bekesy, G. von. (1960). *Experiments in hearing.* New York: McGraw-Hill.

Berliner, J. E. (1973). *Intensity discrimination in audition.* Ph.D. Thesis, Massachusetts Institute of Technology.

Berliner, J. E., & Durlach, N. I. (1973). Intensity perception. IV. Resolution in roving-level discrimination. *Journal of the Acoustical Society of America, 53,* 1270–1287.

Blackman, R. B., & Tukey, J. W. (1959). The measurement of power spectra from the viewpoint of communications engineering. New York: Dover. Reprinted from *Bell System Technical Journal, 37,* 1958.

Braida, L. D., & Durlach, N. I. (1972). Intensity perception. II. Resolution in one-interval paradigms. *Journal of the Acoustical Society of America, 51,* 483–502.

Bucklein, R. (1981). The audibility of frequency response irregularities. *Journal of the Audio Engineering Society, 29,* 126–131.

Buus, S. (1985). Release from masking caused by envelope fluctuations. *Journal of the Acoustical Society of America, 78,* 1958–1965.

Callahan, D. J., Braida, L. D., & Durlach, N. I. (1973). Unpublished data.

Campbell, R. A. (1966). Auditory intensity perception and neural coding. *Journal of the Acoustical Society of America, 39,* 1030–1033.

Campbell, R. A., & Lasky, E. Z. (1967). Masker level and sinusoidal-signal detection. *Journal of the Acoustical Society of America, 42,* 972–976.

Cohen, M., & Schubert, E. Personal communication 1986.

Cooper, G. R., & McGillem, C. D. (1967). *Methods of signal and system analysis.* New York: Holt, Rinehart and Winston.

Dimmick, F. L., & Olson, R. M. (1941). The intensive difference limen in audition. *Journal of the Acoustical Society of America, 12,* 517–525.

Durlach, N. I. (1963). Equalization and cancellation theory of binaural masking level differences. *Journal of the Acoustical Society of America, 35,* 1206–1218.

Durlach, N. I., & Braida, L. D. (1969). Intensity perception. I. Preliminary theory of intensity resolution. *Journal of the Acoustical Society of America, 46,* 372–383.

Durlach, N. I., Braida, L. D., & Ito, Y. (1986). Toward a model for discrimination of broadband signals. *Journal of the Acoustical Society of America, 80,* 63–72.

Evans, E. F. (1974). The effects of hypoxia on the tuning of single cochlear nerve fibers. *Journal of Physiology, 238,* (1), 65–67.

Evans, E. F., & Palmer, A. R. (1980). Relationship between the dynamic range of cochlear nerve fibers and their spontaneous activity. *Experimental Brain Research, 40*, 115–118.

Feth, L. L. (1972). Combinations of amplitude and frequency differences in auditory discrimination. *Acustica, 26*, 67–77.

Feth, L. L. (1974). Frequency discrimination of complex periodic tones. *Perception and Psychophysics, 15*, 375–378.

Feth, L. L. (1986). Personal communication.

Feth, L. L., & O'Malley, H. (1977). Two-tone auditory spectral resolution. *Journal of the Acoustical Society of America, 62*, 940–947.

Feth, L. L., O'Malley, H., & Ramsey, J. Jr. (1982). Pitch of unresolved, two-component complex tones. *Journal of the Acoustical Society of America, 72*, 1403–1412.

Feth, L. L., & Stover, L. J. (1987). Demodulation process in auditory perception. In W. A. Yost & C. S. Watson (Eds.), *Auditory Processing of Complex Sounds.* Hillsdale, NJ: Lawrence Erlbaum Associates.

Fletcher, H. (1940). Auditory patterns. *Review of Modern Physics, 12*, 47–65.

Florentine, M. (1983). Intensity discrimination as a function of level and frequency and its relation to high-frequency hearing. *Journal of the Acoustical Society of America, 74*, 1375–1379.

Florentine, M. (1986). Level discrimination of tones as a function of duration. *Journal of the Acoustical Society of America, 79*, 792–798.

Florentine, M., & Buus, S. (1981). An excitation-pattern model for intensity discrimination. *Journal of the Acoustical Society of America, 70*, 1646–1654.

Galambos, R., & Davis, H. (1943). The response of single auditory-nerve fibers to acoustic stimulation. *Journal of Neurophysiology, 6*, 39–57.

Garner, W. R., & Miller, G. A. (1944). Differential sensitivity to intensity as a function of the duration of the comparison tone. *Journal of Experimental Psychology, 34*, 450–463.

Grantham, D. W. & Yost, W. A. (1982). Measures of intensity discrimination. *Journal of the Acoustical Society of America, 72*, 406–410.

Green, D. M. (1958). Detection of multiple component signals in noise. *Journal of the Acoustical Society of America, 30*, 904–911.

Green, D. M. (1976). *An introduction to hearing.* Hillsdale, NJ: Lawrence Erlbaum Associates.

Green, D. M., & Kidd, G., Jr. (1983). Further studies of auditory profile analysis. *Journal of the Acoustical Society of America, 73*, 1260–1265.

Green, D. M., Kidd, G., Jr., & Picardi, M. C. (1983). Successive versus simultaneous comparison in auditory intensity discrimination. *Journal of the Acoustical Society of America, 73*, 639–643.

Green, D. M., & Mason, C. R. (1985). Auditory profile analysis: Frequency, phase, and Weber's law. *Journal of the Acoustical Society of America, 77*, 1155–1161.

Green, D. M., Mason, C. R., & Kidd, G., Jr. (1984). Profile analysis: Critical bands and duration. *Journal of the Acoustical Society of America, 75*, 1163–1167.

Green, D. M., & Swets, J. A. (1966). *Signal detection theory and psychophysics.* New York: Wiley. (Reprinted by R. E. Krieger, Huntington, NY, 1974.)

Hafter, E. R., & Carrier, S. C. (1970). Masking-level differences obtained with a pulsed tonal masker. *Journal of the Acoustical Society of America, 47*, 1041–1047.

Hall, J. W. (1986). The effect of across-frequency differences in masking level on spectro-temporal pattern analysis. *Journal of the Acoustical Society of America, 79*, 781–787.

Hall, J. W., Haggard, M. P., & Fernandes, M. A. (1984). Detection in noise by spectro-temporal pattern analysis. *Journal of the Acoustical Society of America, 76,* 50–56.

Hanna, T. E., von Gierke, S. M., & Green, D. M. (1986). Detection and intensity discrimination of a sinusoid. *Journal of the Acoustical Society of America, 80,* 1335–1340.

Harris, J. D. (1963). Loudness discrimination. *Journal of Speech and Hearing Disorders,* Monograph Supplement II, 1963.

Haughey, P. J. (1970). *Intensity resolution in audition.* S.B. Thesis, Massachusetts Institute of Technology.

Hawkins, J. E., & Stevens S. S. (1950). The masking of pure tones and of speech by white noise. *Journal of the Acoustical Society of America, 22,* 6–13.

Henning, G. B. (1970). Comparison of the effects of signal duration on frequency and amplitude discrimination. In R. Plomp & G. F. Smoorenburg (Eds.), *Frequency analysis and periodicity detection in hearing.* Leiden: A. W. Sijthoff.

Jesteadt, W., Wier, C. C., & Green, D. M. (1977). Intensity discrimination as a function of frequency and sensation level. *Journal of the Acoustical Society of America, 61,* 169–177.

Johnson, D. H., & Swami, A. (1983). The transmission of signals by auditory-nerve fiber discharge patterns. *Journal of the Acoustical Society of America, 74,* 493–501.

Johnston, R. C. (1972). *Aural intensity resolution near threshold.* S. B. Thesis, Massachusetts Institute of Technology.

Jones, K., Tubis, A., & Burns, E. M., (1985). On the extraction of the signal-excitation function from a non-Poisson cochlear neural spike train. *Journal of the Acoustical Society of America, 78,* 90–94.

Kiang, N. Y.-S. (1965). *Discharge patterns of single fibers in the cat's auditory nerve.* Research Monograph 35, Cambridge, MA: MIT Press.

Kiang, N. Y.-S. (1968). A survey of recent developments in the study of auditory physiology. *Annals of Otology, Rhinology, and Laryngology, 77,* 1–20.

Kidd, G., Jr., Mason, C. R., & Green, D. M. (1986). Auditory profile analysis of irregular sound spectra. *Journal of the Acoustical Society of America, 79,* 1045–1053.

Laming D. (1985). Some principles of sensory analysis. *Psychological Review, 92,* 462–485.

Laming D. J. (1986). *Sensory analysis* London: Academic Press.

Leshowitz, B., & Wightman, F. L. (1971). On-frequency masking with continuous sinusoids. *Journal of the Acoustical Society of America, 49,* 1180–1190.

Liberman, M. C. (1978). Auditory-nerve response from cats raised in a low-noise chamber. *Journal of the Acoustical Society of America, 63,* 442–455.

Luce, R. D., & Green, D. M. (1974). Neural coding and psychophysical discrimination data. *Journal of the Acoustical Society of America, 56,* 1554–1564.

Mason, C. R., Kidd, G., Jr., Hanna, T. E., & Green, D. M. (1984). Profile analysis and level variation. *Hearing Research, 13,* 269–275.

McFadden, D. Personal communication 1986.

McGill, W. J. & Goldberg, J. P. (1986a). A study of the near-miss involving Weber's law and pure-tone intensity discrimination. *Perception & Psychophysics, 4,* 105–109.

McGill, W. J., & Goldberg, J. P. (1968b). Pure-tone intensity discrimination and energy detection. *Journal of the Acoustical Society of America, 44,* 576–581.

Miller, G. A. (1947). Sensitivity to changes in the intensity of white noise and its relation to masking and loudness. *Journal of the Acoustical Society of America, 19,* 609–619.

Moore, B. C. J., & Raab, D. H. (1974). Pure-tone intensity discrimination: Some experiments relative to the "near-miss" to Weber's law. *Journal of the Acoustical Society of America, 55,* 1049–1054.

Moore, B. C. J., & Raab, D. H. (1975). Intensity discrimination for noise bursts in the presence of a continuous, bandstop background: Effects of level, width of the bandstop, and duration. *Journal of the Acoustical Society of America, 57,* 400–405.

Neff, D. L. & Green, D. M. (1987). Effect of number of components and spectral uncertainty on masking by multicomponent maskers. *Perception & Psychophysics, 41,* 409–415.

Patterson, R. (1974). Auditory filter shape. *Journal of the Acoustical Society of America, 55,* 802–809.

Patterson, R. (1976). Auditory filter shape derived with noise stimuli. *Journal of the Acoustical Society of America, 59,* 640–654.

Palmer, A. R., & Evans, E. F. (1982). Intensity coding in the auditory periphery of the cat: Responses of cochlear nerve and cochlear nucleus neurons to signals in the presence of bandstop masking noise. *Hearing Research, 7,* 305–323.

Penner, M. J., Leshowitz, B., Cudahy, E., & Ricard, G. (1974). Intensity discrimination for pulsed sinusoids of various frequencies. *Perception & Psychophysics, 15,* 568–570.

Peterson, W. W., Birdsall, T. G., & Fox, W. C. (1954). The theory of signal detectability. *Professional Group on Information Theory.* PGIT-4, 171–212.

Pillsbury, W. B. (1910). Method for the determination of the intensity of sound in psychological monographs, *Report of the Committee of the American Psychological Association on the Standardizing of Procedures in Experimental Tests, XIII,* 5–20.

Pollack, I. (1955). "Long-time" differential intensity sensitivity. *Journal of the Acoustical Society of America, 27,* 380–381.

Rabinowitz, W. M. (1970). *Frequency and intensity resolution in audition.* S.M. Thesis, Massachusetts Institute of Technology.

Rabinowitz, W. M., Lim, J. S., Braida, L. D., & Durlach, N. I. (1976). Intensity perception. VI. Summary of recent data on deviations from Weber's law for 1000-Hz tone pulses. *Journal of the Acoustical Society of America, 59,* 1506–1509.

Rayleigh, Baron (Strutt, J. W.). (1945). *Theory of sound, Vol. 1.* New York: Dover. (Originally published 1877.)

Richards, W. (1979). Quantify sensory channels: Generalizing colorimetry to orientation and texture, touch and tones. *Sensory Processes, 3,* 207–229.

Riesz, R. R. (1928). Differential sensitivity of the ear for pure tones. *Physical Review, 31,* 867–875.

Rose, J. E., Brugge, J. F., Anderson, D. J., & Hind, J. E. (1967). Phase-locked response to low-frequency tones in single auditory nerve fibers of the squirrel monkey. *Journal of Neurophysiology, 30,* 769–793.

Rose, J. E., Hind, J. E., Anderson, D. J., & Brugge, J. F. (1971). Some effects of stimulus intensity on response of auditory nerve fibers in the squirrel monkey. *Journal of Neurophysiology, 34,* 685–699.

Sachs, M. B., & Abbas, P. J. (1974). Rate versus level functions for auditory-nerve fibers in cats: Tone-burst stimuli. *Journal of the Acoustical Society of America, 56,* 1835–1847.

Sachs, M. B., & Young, E. D. (1979). Encoding of steady-state vowels in the auditory nerve: Representation in terms of discharge rate. *Journal of the Acoustical Society of America, 66,* 470–479.

Schachknow, P. N., & Raab, D. H. (1973). Intensity discrimination of tone bursts and the form of the Weber function. *Perception & Psychophysics, 14,* 449–450.

Scharf, B. (1970). Critical bands. In J. Tobias (Ed.), *Foundations of modern auditory theory* (pp. 159–202). Vol. 1. New York: Academic Press.

Sorkin, R. D. (1966). Temporal interference effects in auditory amplitude discrimination. *Perception & Psychophysics, 1,* 55–58.

Spiegel, M. F., & Green, D. M. (1982). Signal and masker uncertainty with noise maskers of varying duration, bandwidth, and center frequency. *Journal of the Acoustical Society of America, 71,* 1204–1210.

Spiegel, M. F., Picardi, M. C., & Green, D. M. (1981). Signal and masker uncertainty in intensity discrimination. *Journal of the Acoustical Society of America, 70,* 1015–1019.

Stevens, S. S. (1975). *Psychophysics: Introduction to its perceptual, neural, and social prospects.* New York: Wiley.

Stover, L. J., & Feth, L. L. (1983). Pitch of narrow-band signals. *Journal of the Acoustical Society of America, 73,* 1701–1707.

Swets, J. A., Green, D. M. & Tanner, W. P., Jr. (1962). On the width of the critical band. *Journal of the Acoustical Society of America, 34,* 108–113.

Tanner, W. P., Jr. (1961). Physiological implications of psychophysical data. *Annual of the N.Y. Academy of Science, 89,* 752–765.

Teich, M. C., & Khanna, S. M. (1985). Pulse-number distribution for the neural spike train in the cat's auditory nerve. *Journal of the Acoustical Society of America, 77,* 1110–1128.

Teich, M. C., & Lachs, G. (1979). A neural-counting model incorporating refractoriness and spread of excitation. *Journal of the Acoustical Society of America, 66,* 1738–1749.

van de Geer, J. P. (1971). *Introduction to multivariate analysis for the social sciences.* San Francisco: W. H. Freeman and Company.

Viemeister, N. F. (1972). Intensity discrimination of pulsed sinusoids: The effects of filtered noise. *Journal of the Acoustical Society of America, 51,* 1265–1269.

Viemeister, N. F. (1982). Auditory intensity discrimination at high frequencies in the presence of noise. *Science, 221,* 1206–1208.

Viemeister, N. F. (1984). Personal communication.

Voelcker, H. B. (1966a). Toward a unified theory of modulation—Part II: Zero manipulation. *Proceedings of the IEEE, 54,* 735–755.

Voelcker, H. B. (1966b). Toward a unified theory of modulation—Part I: Phase-envelope relationships. *Proceedings of the IEEE, 54,* 340–353.

Watson, C. S. (1976). Factors in the discrimination of word-length auditory patterns. In S. K. Hirsch, D. H. Eldredge, I. J. Hirsch, and S. R. Silverman (Eds.), *Hearing and Davis: Essays honoring Hallowell Davis* (pp. 175–189). St. Louis: Washington University Press.

Watson, C. S., Kelly, W. J., & Wroton, H. W. (1976). Factors in the discrimination of tonal patterns. II. Selective attention and learning under various levels of stimulus uncertainty. *Journal of the Acoustical Society of America, 60,* 1176–1186.

Watson, C. S., Wroton, H. W., Kelly, W. J., & Benbassat, C. A. (1975). Factors in the discrimination on tonal patterns: I. Component frequency, temporal position, and silent intervals. *Journal of the Acoustical Society of America, 57,* 1175–1185.

Weber, D. L. (1978). Suppression and critical bands in band-limiting experiments. *Journal of the Acoustical Society of America, 64,* 141–150.

Wegel, R. L., & Lane, C. E. (1924). The auditory masking of one pure tone by another and its probable relation to the dynamics of the inner ear. *Physical Review, 23,* 266–285.

Whitfield, I. C. (1967). *The auditory pathway.* London: Edward Arnold.

Young, E. D., & Barta, P. E. (1986). Rate responses of auditory nerve fibers to tones in noise near masked threshold. *Journal of the Acoustical Society of America, 79,* 426–442.

Young, E. D., & Sachs, M. B. (1979). Representation of steady-state vowels in the temporal aspects of the discharge patterns of populations of auditory-nerve fibers. *Journal of the Acoustical Society of America, 66,* 1381–1403.

Zwicker, E. (1958). Über psychologische und methodische Grundlagen der Lautheit. *Acustica,* Acustishe Beihefte I, 237–258.

Zwicker, E. (1970). Masking and psychological excitation as consequences of the ear's frequency analysis. In R. Plomp and G. F. Smooremburg (Eds.), *Frequency analysis and periodicity detection in hearing.* (pp. 376–396) Leiden: A. W. Sijhoff.

Zwicker, E., & Henning, G. B. (1985). The four factors leading to binaural masking-level differences. *Hearing Research, 19,* 29–47.

Zwislocki, J. J., & Jordan, H. N. (1986). On the relation of intensity jnd's to loudness and neural noise. *Journal of the Acoustical Society of America, 79,* 772–780.

Index